# A Brief and Truthful Description
# of a Journey to and from Guinea

by

## JOHANNES RASK

# TWO VIEWS
# FROM
# CHRISTIANSBORG CASTLE

## Johannes Rask (1708-1713)
## H.C. Monrad (1805-1809)

### Volume I

# A Brief and Truthful Description
# of a Journey to and from Guinea

by

## JOHANNES RASK

**Translated from Danish
by**

## SELENA AXELROD WINSNES

SUB-SAHARAN PUBLISHERS

Published in 2009 by
SUB-SAHARAN PUBLISHERS
P.O. BOX LG358,
LEGON, ACCRA, GHANA

This printing 2017

ISBN: 978-9988-647-89-6

The translation of this publication was
kindly supported by the
DANISH ARTS COUNCIL
H.C. ANDERSEN BOULEVARD 2
DK-1553 COPENHAGEN V

Typesetting and Cover design by
Kwabena Agyepong

In Memory of

Paul Hair

in gratitude
with apologies

# CONTENTS

# List of Illustrations and Maps

# Foreword

When Johannes Rask left Copenhagen for the Gold Coast in November of 1708 he was just thirty years old and newly ordained as a Lutheran priest. Queen Anne was on the throne of England, France and England were at war, and the trans-Atlantic slave trade was about to reach its height. Rask was away from Denmark-Norway for four and a half years, of which three and a half years were spent at Christiansborg Castle, the main Danish establishment on the coast, as chaplain to the castle staff. The rest of the time was taken up in traveling – in those days of total dependence on sail, getting back to Europe from the Gold Coast required going to the West Indies en route, and in any case that is where all the ships from the Coast were bound. It was clearly the adventure of his lifetime, and if nothing else, this "Brief and Truthful Description" drawn from his diaries succeeds in giving today's reader a vivid sense of what it was like to be a European traveling in the tropics in those days, and incidentally of the "cultural baggage" they took with them. Accustomed as we have become to jet travel, treated water and antibiotics, any reader is bound to be struck not just by how long the trip took – about five months from Copenhagen to Christiansborg at Osu near Accra – but by the number of deaths en route among the crew, several before the ship had even reached the tropics, and the danger of pirates, mainly French it seems.

Rask is very particular in noting details related to death and the customs surrounding it, among both Europeans and Africans. Sudden death was obviously an ever present threat to all and an intense preoccupation for Rask personally, heightened by both philosophical inclination and his duties as a priest. His description of the two forms of burial then current in Accra, with a more or less vertical grave in open ground for commoners but under the floor of the house for the aristocracy, is particularly interesting. But funerals are by no means his only topic. Anyone familiar with Accra today will be fascinated by his description of the town (it could hardly then be termed a city) in 1710-12, when Akwamu was the dominant power, and large wild animals inhabited the Accra plain. Rask is not always absolutely certain what kind of animal was involved, but it appears hyenas were known to attack humans in their houses in Dutch Accra. Yet not everything has changed – he also complains of the dirty state of the streets there.

Rask carefully distinguishes what he knows personally from what he gets by hearsay, and notes whom he hears it from, and on several occasions corrects Dapper. Nevertheless we notice that he puts a certain rather strange distance between himself and his subject matter. As a striking example, although he mentions slaves as a matter of course, and the slave trade must have been going on all around him, he does not discuss it until he gets to the Portuguese island of São Thomé on his way back to Europe, where his national loyalties are not engaged. Then he refers to "this abhorrent trade", and describes it as though he had never seen it before (Chapter 35). The ship he was traveling on certainly carried a slave cargo, but he makes no mention of it.

Rask seems never to have ventured far from Christiansborg, apart from occasional visits to other European establishments, and to have spent virtually the entire three and a half years among Europeans, who were of course his main charge and congregation at the Castle. He makes numerous comments on customs at Ouidah ("Fida") and Popo but seems never to have gone there. Although his objective descriptions of events seem generally trustworthy it is fairly clear that he had little real comprehension of what he observed. Many readers will be surprised at his claim that witchcraft did not exist in Accra. Perhaps it was because he could not identify what he heard of with European witchcraft practices, but it is strange nonetheless. Another odd mistake that casts doubt on the extent of his contact with Africans is contained in the list of Akwamu Twi ("Aqvambuish") words in Chapter 19. A few of the words, including those for "tobacco pipe", "knife", "ear", "nose", "mouth", "head", are not Twi at all but Ga. Perhaps part of his problem was that unlike most of his compatriots, he had no local wife! Or if he did he most certainly does not tell us about it. Considering his concern for his position as a priest, as well has his disdainful comments on African marriage in general, it seems unlikely.

Indeed a major feature of his writing that most readers will find hard to stomach is that he seems hardly able to describe any custom or feature of local life without denigrating it, even if his initial impulse is clearly to praise it, and he is sometimes gratuitously insulting, for example in his comments on Homowo, the annual Ga harvest festival. This is largely in the spirit of his age, but it goes beyond what we find in the writings of other·Europeans on the coast. I suggest that his attitudes are also closely connected with how he saw his position as Christian chaplain. He was on the Guinea coast almost a century before the earliest Protestant efforts at evangelizing among Africans, and it is clear that not only was it not part of his official job, he never contemplated the idea. When he meets African practicing Catholics on São Thomé he is oddly non-committal on whether he approves or not. The word "Christian" is for him a synonym for "European". Perhaps he had to continually remind himself of the inherent worthlessness of heathen customs, just in case he found himself being attracted to any of them.

This does not prevent him from citing Biblical parallels for what he saw, no matter how far fetched. He even lists some local names, comparing them with similar Biblical names. He then adds that these similarities are of no consequence, but the urge to find Biblical roots for virtually everything local is with us still today.

Despite his disapproval of almost everything, one gets the impression that he was genuinely sorry to leave. All the tensions and contradictions disappear when Rask gets to England, of which he was a great admirer. As an enthusiastic tourist in London he sounds like many a modern traveler, and reports on many of the same sights.

Selena Axelrod Winsnes is greatly to be thanked for this highly readable volume, the latest from the extensive eighteenth century Danish literature on the Gold Coast that she has so expertly translated. Scholars will be grateful that an informative document on the Guinea coast has at last been made available to those who do not read Danish (or Nynorsk), but it should find a wider readership too. The author's prejudices and limitations did not prevent him from being a keen observer, and the curious general reader, especially anyone familiar with Accra in more recent times, will find it a rewarding source of insights into what life was like here, way back then.

*M.E. Kropp Dakubu*
*Institute of African Studies*
*University of Ghana, Legon. 2008*

# Preface and Acknowledgements

## Two Views from Christiansborg Castle

My personal project of translating and editing the primary Danish sources for the history of Ghana began in 1980, the result of a combination of circumstances – serendipity, if you will. Once the first one was published, requests began to come in for making others available, and it was impossible for me to say 'No'. Thus, my fourth career started when I was fully adult, and it has continued until now, 27 years later, when age is impinging on me.

There remain two books that most certainly should be in the public domain, for the use of scholars and students, as well as lay readers, which I am able to translate without too much trouble:

Johannes Rask *A Brief and Truthful Description of a Journey to and from Guinea 1708-1713)* published posthumously 1754;

H.C. Monrad *A Description of the Guinea Coast and its Inhabitants (1805-1809)* published 1822.

However, extensive editing is now out of the question for me. Thus, with a degree of trepidation, I shall make them available in translation, with only the most necessary, explanatory, footnotes.

My hesitation is based on the fact that such books are frequently read and accepted at face value – they were, after all, eye-witness accounts – but they often cry out for scholarly comment. The authors had read other authors, copied some; they each had their own agenda; they reflected their own times; they launched their own opinions, frequently as a result of misinterpretation. And almost all of them were writing for public consumption, thus a view to the market was always a factor. Exotic, entertaining, even hair-raising glimpses could be welcome in that respect. But they were also intended to be informative, and they did succeed in this.

The present edition, my final contribution in this field, is two-part, as the title suggests. Why not simply publish them as two separate books? Since, for various reasons, the other books in this corpus have not been published, in English, in chronological order of their appearance, I found myself with the last two written with a full century between them. In re-reading them I was struck by a parallel that intrigued me. Here are two men, Johannes Rask and H.C. Monrad, both young, both ministers in the Evangelical Lutheran Church of Denmark-Norway.[1] For each of them this was a first time outside of Europe. Their appointments, as chaplains to the Danish-Norwegian establishment on the Gold Coast, were to serve that staff, and their African wives and children; that is, they were not sent out as missionaries. They were both to reside at *Christiansborg Castle* during their tour of duty. Their education and training were comparable, they had both read other authors who had written about Africa and the West Indies.

However, it is precisely that century between them that makes the great difference.

Johannes Rask arrived on the Gold Coast at the very beginning of the eighteenth century, when the export slave trade was being fully launched. H. C. Monrad was sent out at the beginning of the nineteenth century, just as Denmark-Norway had made active the treaty abolishing the export slave trade. This is reflected in the mind-sets of the two men. As did other authors writing about this area, they reported on much the same things, but their presentation, their attitudes, were worlds apart. The century between the two men was marked by the enormity of the export slave trade, beginning in earnest in Rask's time. As the century wore on, the trade grew gradually less profitable, and the movement towards abolition expanded. In Rask's time the trade in enslaved Africans was legal and acceptable, albeit there were, intermittently, murmurs of moral discomfort. Monrad arrived at the beginning of the

---

1 It seems to be the convention in Denmark to use only the initials H.C. for those two obviously favourite names, Hans Christian. (Cf. H.C. Andersen).

nineteenth century, precisely when that trade had just been abolished by Denmark-Norway – taking effect in 1803 and decreed illegal after that. This, of course, marked the two men. Their thinking, then their writing, grew out of these opposing systems.

To what purpose, then, should these texts be translated and read? Granted that they described much the same things, but they also saw different aspects: where Rask, confronted with 'heathen' worship, and 'worse', sees anomie everywhere, Monrad sees much that deserves respect. Where Rask states flatly that 'music' is totally lacking, Monrad waxes lyrical on hearing a local musician. These are detailed historical and ethnographic reports of two different periods. The history – both European and African – that comprised the background of their experience, as recounted by Rask is far different from that encountered by Monrad. Further, they provide details that give the reader different insights into life and customs on the Gold Coast in those divergent periods: Rask reports on girls jumping 'rope' and burials in an upright position; Monrad describes palavers in great detail. Finally, such books were undoubtedly instrumental in both the creation and the enhancement of images of Africa and Africans – images that may have lingered through generations.

These two books are simultaneously in conflict with, and comple-ment, one another. It appears logical to me that they be considered side-by-side, thus the two-volume edition. Since, however, they are lacking in editorial comment, it is my intention that the translations be treated as the raw material they are.

Because these old texts – in gothic script – are rife with terms that are both highly specialized and archaic, and not easy to find in modern reference materials, I have been fortunate in receiving help from experts in various fields. Always on call is Mary Esther Dakubu for glossing terms in Ghanaian languages. Further, I wish to thank Erik Gøbel for help with Danish expressions and archaic terms; Johan Kloster and Mathias Winsnes, for providing me with nautical terminology. Adam Jones gave me necessary information on Olfert Dapper. Peer Winsnes and Leif Svalesen spared no effort in the acquisition of illustrations. I wish, particularly, to acknowledge help given me in theological matters by Svein Helge Birkeflet; in biology by Kirsten Borse Haraldsen and Irene Lindblad; in history by Finn Fuglestad. Thanks, too, to Tippa Hareide for casting a critical eye over my writing.

Finally, I wish to express my gratitude for a project grant provided by the Norwegian Non-fiction Writers and Translators Association.

If, in spite of all this aid, there appear errors in the texts, the fault is entirely my own.

*Selena Axelrod Winsnes*
*Rælingen, Norway*
*2008*

# Translator's Introduction

*Johannes Rask 1708-1713*

## General background

The eighteenth century opened to a well-functioning system of interaction in trade between Africans and Europeans on the Gold Coast of West Africa [Ghana]. The armed competition between the European nations, seen in the preceding century, was over. African communities along the coast were now accustomed to doing business with Europeans. There was intense activity during the eighteenth century in building lodges and forts, specifically on the Gold Coast, in contrast to the Slave Coast [from Volta River eastward to Lagos]. This was due in large part to geography: the latter coast comprised sandbars and lagoons, whereas the Gold Coast provided rocky headlands suitable for permanent structures. This meant that the Europeans on the Slave Coast, having to build inland and close to the reigning Africans, were more like 'ambassadors'; while those on Gold Coast could be well-established in their forts, as 'embryo colonial governors', able to exercise a degree of control of trade there.[2] Currency systems were well-established in West Africa: cowrie shells on the Slave Coast; gold dust on the Gold Coast – actually in combination precisely in Accra – and both available for implementation in trade with the Europeans, alongside the trade in exchange of goods. Furthermore, due to the heavy surf and breakers the large sailing ships from Europe were unable to come close to land, being forced to anchor in the roads.

---

2    J.D. Fage *A History of Africa*, (1995) 251.

Thus, transportation ship-to-shore by the expert African canoemen and their large dugout canoes was a *sine qua non* for trade.[3]

The ever-increasing demand for slave labour in the plantations in the Americas resulted in the great expansion of the trade in enslaved Africans during the eighteenth century. The use of slave labour was also a well-established aspect of life among the West Africans. Thus the acquisition of enslaved individuals, whether as prisoners of war or by raids, or as debtors, criminals, and 'undesireables', readily provided that 'commodity' – along with gold and ivory, *et al.* – for trade with the Europeans in exchange for goods brought in their ships.[4] Those goods were cloth from both Asia and Europe; iron and manufactured metal objects; muskets; gunpowder and flints; spirits; beads, etc. After two centuries of experience the Africans were well-organized in trade with Europeans. A merchant class was emerging, both of Africans as well as Europeans who married into African families. In several cases these grew into dynasties, some still in existence today. They often sent their sons to Europe for education.

## The Akwamu Empire

The African political situation in the Ga area during Rask's years there was characterized as the height of Akwamu imperial power. Several of the African nations on the Gold Coast were constantly jockeying for positions of power, seeking, in particular, control of the coastal trade: both that of traditional trade for salt and dried fish, as well as trade with the European ships. Akwamu, had started its expansion in the second half of the seventeenth century, and by the onset of the eighteenth century that empire held sway over an area from Accra, inland to include Akuapem, and eastward, across the Volta River, well into Dahomey. Accra had been conquered in 1677-81. The Akwamu capital was probably Nynanaoase. The Danish Lieutenant Erik Tilleman describes life under the Akwamu at the end of the seventeenth

---

3    See the painting that illustrates this system.

4    For a description of the various grades of slavery, and their mode of enslavement, see I. Wilks *Akwamu 1640-1750* (2001) 73.

century. This includes machinations on the part of the Accra [Ga] to cheat the Akwamu in trade.[5] The possession of muskets was of the utmost importance in achieving not only power, but prestige; and the Europeans showed no hesitation in providing that component.

One of the most spectacular actions of the Akwamu was the capture of Christiansborg Castle in 1693. This, however, was not dependent upon superior power, but was accomplished by a ruse effected by a single man – Asameni – leading a group of so-called merchants. The 'merchants', ostensibly there to purchase muskets, had been welcomed into the Castle grounds. They were given the muskets for examination, but, having hidden powder and shot under their clothing, they managed to load them. The staff at the Castle were badly manhandled, and the Akwamu took over control.[6] They held the Castle, with Asameni in charge, for a year; after which they returned it to the Danes for payment of 50 marks of gold, as well as agreeing not to demand reparations for losses incurred. However, they kept the keys to the Castle, which are now stool property in Akwamu.[7]

In 1703 King Akwonno (1702-1725) negotiated a treaty with the Dutch – whose Fort Crèvecoeur was a close neighbour to Christiansborg. The terms acknowledged Akwamu sovereignty over Accra; bound the Dutch to assist Akwamu with men and arms in future 'just' wars; bound the Dutch to pay monthly rental for Fort Crèvecoeur plus a percentage of gold traded from that fort. Akwamu, in turn, agreed to keep trade routes to the interior open, bound his chiefs not to act in any way that would interfere with the trade; promised to prevent his subjects from trading with interlopers instead of the fort; and promised not to engage in wars that would damage the trade.[8] An example of what an African power could do is seen when, in 1700, the Akwamu King Ado prevented merchants from going to Danish Christiansborg bcause he had heard that a Danish ship had sold muskets to enemies of

---

5    See Erick Tilleman *A Short and Simple Account...1697...*(1994) Chapter Seven.

6    For various versions of what happened during and immediately after the take-over of Christiansborg Castle, see *ibid* 16, n.144.

7    See the photograph of the keys.

8    See Wilks, *op.cit.* 33.

Akwamu.[9] Europeans repeatedly stated that they would remain neutral in conflicts between African nations; that they were there to trade, not to indulge in politics. In practise, however, this stand was frequently ignored; pragmatism coming to the fore. The African nations could, at any time, block, or close, the routes to the interior. They provided – or refused to provide – foodstuffs, water, firewood, to supplement what was brought in the ships from Europe – and ships from Denmark were notoriously few and far between. African traders brought the trade goods to the coast, and could choose whether to trade with the forts or with interlopers. Thus, the Europeans living in the forts and castles had, of real necessity, to accommodate the Africans. Equally important for the Africans were the income derived from monthly rental from the forts; military support in the event of war; places of refuge within the forts and castles during enemy attack; and the goods brought from Europe – with muskets taking pride of place for those at war.

As noted above, the Akwamu empire was at the height of its power during this period, and continued so until the second and third decades of the century. But Akwamu rule had gradually become more oppressive. Growing discontent among its subject peoples combined with the hatred of traditional enemies, led by the Akim. Opponents to the rule even included a number of the Akwamu who were chafing under a cruel system. The insatiable demand for slaves for the West Indian plantations had now had the effect that Africans from all walks of life were being seized by Akwamu raiders, not just those 'traditionally' enslaved. In 1708 – the year of Rask's arrival on the Coast – the Danish Governor Lygård's declaration of neutrality in the conflict was belied by his constantly providing the Akwamu with guns and ammunition. The trade was welcome.

Open rebellions and armed conflicts began in 1727 and continued for the next three years. The Danes and Dutch in the Accra area were drawn into the fray but reacted very differently: the former showing good will; the latter hostility.[10] The demise of Akwamu sovereignty

---

9   *Ibid* p. 49.

10   In 1727 the Akwamu King was Ansa Kwao; the Danish Governor was A.P.Wærøe; the Dutch factor at Crèvecoeur was de la Planque.

came in 1730, after a series of battles, blockades by the Akwamu of the Dutch and English forts on the coast, treaties made and broken. All of this is described in rich detail by another Dane, L.F. Rømer whose stay at Christiansborg started just short of a decade after that defeat and the removal of Akwamu from the coast – they settled in a small area, inland, on the banks of the Volta River.[11] The story, still fresh in memory, was told to him by a Ga chief priest, who was his friend.

## Christiansborg Castle

The site, in Osu, on which Christiansborg Castle was built was purchased from the King of Accra by the Danes in 1661. The Danish headquarters were located in Fetu country at that time – that is, Frederiksborg Fort on Amanful Hill, overlooking Cape Coast Castle. Experiencing serious economic problems in the 1680s, and deeply in debt to the English at Cape Coast, the Danish governor found it necessary first to pawn, then to sell, the fort to the English who were in command at Cape Coast Castle. This was in 1685. The Danes then removed to their already existing Fort Christiansborg in Accra. This fort was enlarged during the following years, to become the Castle and headquarters for the Danish establishments on the Gold Coast. It comprised the residence for the Danish staff; the warehouse for trade goods; the chapel; a school; dungeons for criminals and slaves. The courtyard was used as a market for the international trade; for ceremonies; for the placement of the vital cistern; and for a place of refuge for the Africans living around the Castle in times of war.

Christiansborg fell into the hands of other nations on two occasions. The Portuguese held it, as Fort St. Francis Xavier, from 1679-1683; and, as noted above, the Akwamu held it from 1693-94. In the course of the following years the fort was greatly enlarged and its appearance has changed drastically through time. Albert van Dantzig gives us

---

11    See L.F. Rømer *A Reliable Account of the Cost of Guinea (1760)* (2000) for the rise and fall of the Akwamu kingdom 116-137. See also Wilks, Chapter Three for the collapse of Akwamu.

three images showing extreme change through three centuries.[12] Sold to the English in 1850 – together with all the other Danish possessions – it became the headquarters of the Republic of Ghana, which status it retains to this day. However, I hear, at the present writing, that the government headquarters will be moved to a more suitable building, and that the Castle may become the museum it should be.

## Johannes Rask on the Coast

At the time of Rask's arrival on the Coast in 1709, the Danish Governor was Eric Olsen Lygaard, who was serving his second term as governor – the first was February to December 1698; the second was May 1705 to Aug 1711. Precisely at the time of Rask's arrival at Christiansborg Lygaard had placed himself in an impossible situation. Settlements around the Castle were being attacked by the Akwamu, and the inhabitants rushed to seek refuge in the Castle grounds. Lygaard refused them entry, stating that his job was to remain neutral – all the while he was providing the Akwamu with muskets and powder. The Africans outside the Castle were massacred. Thus Lygaard's position, both among the Africans and the Europeans, had become untenable, and he sent a request to Copenhagen to be relieved of his post. However, he continued as governor until 1711. During these last two years of his appointment he had to placate the King of Akwamu [Aquando] a number of times. Animosity against Lygaard grew apace, and the leader of the opposition was none other than Johannes Rask, for personal reasons. Evidently Lygaard had accused Rask of indulging in private trade, which he felt was not compatible with his position as chaplain, and, according to a Danish historian, he confiscated part of Rask's property.[13] However, Rask retained his position until September 1712, when he departed for home for reasons of poor health. Lygaard was relieved of his office in August 1711, and a successor, Frantz Boye, had been sent to replace him.[14] Upon Bøye's arrival, Lygaard, now ill,

---

12    Albert van Dantzig, *Forts and Castles of Ghana* (1980) 30.

13    Georg Nørregård *Danish Settlements in West Africa 1658-1850* (1966) 69.

14    Frantz Boye remained as governor until November 1717.

'shut himself up and died shortly after'.[15] Remarks in Rask's text indicate that he and Boye became friends – perhaps having a common interest in their opposition to Lygaard. None of this conflict is mentioned in Rask's text, published after his death. Either he himself made no mention of it in his diary, or removed it; or it was removed by his son or by Bishop Nannestad, who published the book.

The only biographical information about Rask (1678-1744) that I have been able to find is derived from the epilogue to the text, written by Frideric Nannestad, Bishop in Trondheim, who published Rask's material in 1754, ten years after his death. Thus, it has been included after the main text, as in the original edition. The Bishop's prologue, however, is a small treatise in itself – comprising 54 p. 8°. Here Nannestad tells how, on a visitation, he was given the manuscript by Rask's son, nine years after Rask's death. The son told him that his father had intended the material to be published, but, as Nannestad explains, there were physical hindrances: the city of Trondheim had no printers and to have it published in Copenhagen would have required long and difficult communication. The Bishop goes on to justify his publishing the work, since it had been given to him by Rask's son for that purpose – lest he be accused of not having acquired it legally. He also explained why he considered it worth the expense and trouble to publish it. He remarks that many travel texts were written by people with special interests: merchants who were interested in business; sailors writing about the sea and voyages; military persons reporting on warfare; writers of fiction and fantasy producing books which he considered useless. But here was a minister who wrote of serious matters, and in a manner which would be edifying to the ordinary reader. However, Nannestad uses Rask's biblical references to expound at great length on theological matters – citing numerous other writers on these themes. I have not found this to be germane to the text, as regards African studies, so I have not included any of it.

---

15  Nørregård (1966)69.

## The translation

The original edition was printed in Danish gothic script. The text is 313 p. 8°. There is an index of 47 p. 8° not included in this edition, but I have made one of my own. I have kept the translation as close to the original as possible, but have had to reconstruct some of the long latinate sentences for easier reading. Capitalization of nouns has been omitted. The book was written as a diary, basically, but there were long inserts on various subjects throughout, as they occurred to him, so I have supplied chapter divisions for greater ease in finding these. All (–) are the author's; editorial comment is in [–]. The orthography of proper names is as the author wrote them.

To the best of my knowledge there is only one other translation of this book, comprising Rask's own text and an index. It is *Ferd til og frå Guinea 1708-1713*, Jostein R. Øvrelid, Oslo 1969, in *Nynorsk*[16].

---

16  *Nynorsk* [New Norwegian] has been the second official language in Norway since 1929. It is a language constructed to combine Norwegian dialects, originally called *Landsmål* [Country Language].

# A BRIEF AND TRUTHFUL
# DESCRIPTION OF A JOURNEY
## TO AND FROM
# GUINEA

Compiled by

# Mr. JOHANNES RASK
*Formerly Chaplain at Christiansborg Castle*
*Latterly Vicar in Rorstad in Nordland*

**Tronhjem 1754**

# Table of Contents

# Chapter One

'The earth is the Lord's and all therein: the kingdom of earth and all that live on it': *Psal*.24.1

'For here have we no continuing city, but seek one to come. / By him therefore let us offer the sacrifice of praise to God continually, that is, the fruit of our lips giving thanks to his name.' *Hebrews* 13: 14,15

In the year **1708**, on the 6 October, in the name of the Lord, I was called by the Directors in Copenhagen, of the West-Indian and Guinea Company, His Excellency Mr. Matth. Moth and Messrs. Rhode, Becher, Lerke and Schup, to be the garrison priest at the Royal Castle Christiansborg, in Accra, in Guinea, Africa.

On 19 October I was confirmed in this calling most graciously by his Majesty, under his hand and seal.

Thereupon, on the last day of that month, 31 October, in the Church of Our Lady in Copenhagen, //2// I was ordained for this holy office by His Excellency D. Henrik Borneman, Bishop of the Zealand diocese, with prayers and the laying on of hands.

On 22 November, I had my belongings carried on board the ship *Friderik 4th*, and then we lay weather-bound in the road at Copenhagen until 5 December, when, with a light breeze, we weighed anchor. We were forced to drop anchor at Humlebek [Humlebæk] in the evening.

On the 6th we weighed anchor again, and arrived within a half-mile of Krognborg [Kronborg Castle].

The 21st we were under sail again, and passed Krognborg at about 10:30 in the morning. In the afternoon, at 3 o'clock, we had Kulden on one side, and at night, with easy sailing, we passed Niddingen and Anholt.

On the 14th we sailed past Norway's most southerly point, Lindesnæs [Lindesnes], and saw no land before the 18th of the same month, when, at midday, we saw the northern part of *Hetland* southeast of us.[1] We had easy sailing and an accommodating wind. //3// On the same day, at 10:00 in the morning, one of the sloop rowers died; and at the stroke of 12, under a flag waving at half mast, and with a single cannon shot, he was lowered overboard – after we had held confession of our trusting hope of that body's honourable resurrection; had [professed] to divine remembrance of our mortality; and made preparations for a blessed Christian departure – having earlier sung a funeral song. In the evening, between 8 and 9 o'clock, our barber, Peter Vollenberg, died, who, on the morning of the 19th, after prayers, was lowered overboard.

The 20th to 25th we had constant storms and bad weather.

In the evening of the 1st day of Christmas, at about 8 o'clock, we had such a torrential rain astern that our Chief Bosun, Søren Hansøn, was swept overboard and disappeared. Two other men who had been working with him, shared the same fate but were miraculously rescued, undoubtedly with the help of God. Of all the hardship and danger we experienced during the entire journey out, nothing affected us as deeply as this. Beside the fact that the ship was very unstable on the starboard side, and heeled over easily in a light breeze, it was very heavily overloaded, //4// and the sea washed over the boat with such great force that the port arm on which the sheet-anchor rested, broke apart and the anchors fell down in the bow.[2] Our barge, which was fastened above the main hatch, was swamped, so the 3 or 4 pigs we had had to keep there because of the constant storms and torrential rains, were swimming, and were nearly washed overboard; had not the yawl, which was bound fast above the barge, prevented such a departure. On the yawl the entire starboard railing had broken from its timbers by that same heavy sea. We had stowed our mainsail before nightfall, which was lucky for us, yet the ship lay for a long time before it could

---

1   Ships sailing from Denmark to the North Sea regularly sailed northward first, to skirt the coast of Norway where there were safe harbours, in the event of an emergency, in contrast to the sand banks along the northern coast of Denmark. *Hetland/Hjætland* is the old Scandinavian term for the Shetland Islands.

2   A sheet-anchor is the largest of the ship's anchors; used only in emergencies.

be righted; and the water level on deck was so high that all the cannon ports were kept closed, and the scuppers could not remove the water very quickly.

From 25 December until New Year's Day we had such violent storms constantly that we could not hold religious services.

From 1 January **1709** the same constant storm continued without cessation until 12 January. Then another one of our men, Jeppe Rasmusøn, died. The weather began to //**5**// change somewhat for the better, after we had suffered sufficient fear and anxiety.

On the 13th we estimated that we had reached Barles eller Barlinges, so, on that day, everyone on the ship who had not sailed past this point before was initiated.[3] The buckets [of seawater] were employed so energetically that few went to bed dry, and the apprentices had been well and truly baptized.

On the 16th, at about 1:00 in the afternoon, at a couple of degrees north of the Canary Islands, we saw a small sailer whose course was northeast, but when he sighted us quite clearly, he veered off to the west, toward us. Immediately the yards were fastened in their chains, all the bulkheads were made ready, and under our pennant and the royal Danish flag, a 6-pounder was fired with live ammunition, to show him that we were free men, whereupon he quickly hoisted his sail and sailed away from us, heading northeast.[4] By all appearances it was a small Turk, since he did not want to show his colours.

On the 30th of the same month, at 5th glass during the day watch, our Constable, Ole Romstad, a Norwegian, died.[5] He was lowered

---

3    It is difficult to know what R. means by 'Barlinges'. He might mean that they estimate they are at the latitude of the Balearic Islands. But that would be so far north, considering they reached the Canary Islands three days later, that a ritual initiation would not be appropriate. The initiation evidently occurred when crossing the Tropic of Cancer, which would be much farther south. Rask may have had his notes mixed up. For a description of such initiations, and references, see *Letters on West Africa and the Slave Trade: Paul Erdmann Isert's Journey...(1788)* 1992: 24-5; idem 2007: 39-41.

4    The yard, in nautical terminology, is the thin rod, or spar, fastened at right angles to the mast, to support the sail.

5    The watch system, and terminology, differed between nations. Here we shall use the Scandinavian system: first/evening watch: 2000 to midnight; dog watch: midnight to 0400; day watch: 0400 to 0800; morning watch: 0800 to 1400; afternoon watch: 1400 to 2000. (p.c.. Johan Kloster.)

overboard on the same day. When the 6ᵗʰ glass of the day watch was over we sighted land on //6// the Barbary Coast. That country – which I have called the Barbary since I did not know the name of the kingdom – must have been the kingdom Zenega [Senegal], within whose boundaries must lay Capo Verde, according to Dapper.⁶ This is probably true, since, in the early morning of the day after we first sighted it – although without [the help of] a southerly breeze, but sailing mostly by the current – we could see Our Lady's Breasts, which are two round, raised hills, slightly separated; and at 10 bells in the morning we sailed into the Bay of Capo Verde. Regardless of what it is called, it is a delightful flat land reaching out to the edge of the sea, and the sand at the shore is so glittering that in the clear sunshine it seems to sparkle before your eyes.

**1709**, 2 February. At 10:00 in the morning we arrived at Capo Verde, or 'the green head', which is a headland, stretching far out to sea, but mountainous; on whose summit, as well as at the base, the French have their forts. This is not the mainland, but a small island, lying such that they are able to fire on any ship coming from either north or south before entering the bay. They have enough space on the island to be able to //7// keep sufficient cattle to provision those at the forts for a long time; and they have no need of taking their boats or fishing nets farther out to sea than where they can pull them in with lines at 30 or 40 fathoms depth, and thus, daily, catch fish in great quantities. There were 6 canoes carrying fish alongside before we anchored, and we bought a good-sized bream for 1 shilling. This variety of bream – which the Negroes down on the Gold Coast, where the Danish fortress

---

6    Olfert Dapper (1635/1636-1689) spent his whole life in the Netherlands and published
     a large number of geographical works on various parts of the world. His book on Africa,
     published in Amsterdam in 1668 (2nd. Edition 1676, German translation 1670) made
     use of many printed works in various languages, but also included important material on
     West, West Central and South Africa derived from unpublished sources which no longer
     exist, some of it dating from the first half of the seventeenth century. (Adam Jones,
     'Decompiling Dapper: A preliminary search for existence' *History in Africa* 17 (1990)
     171-209; *idem* 'Olfert Dapper et sa description de l'Afrique' in *Objets Interdits* (Paris
     1989) 73-84, 87.) The edition Rask cites throughout his text is probably the German
     translation: *Umbeständliche und eigentliche Beschreibung von Afrika*, Amsterdam 1670.

Christiansborg lies, call *sinkesu* – looks the same as, and tastes as good, as the bream in Denmark.[7] Yet it should be noted that those all along that coast have red scales and skin, but the fish itself is lovely white meat. At Christiansborg it is only found in June, July and August, and it is far better than that caught at Capo Verde, where all the fish tastes very muddy, doubtless because of the sea bed.

In the same harbour we encountered the frigate *Guldenlev*, bound for Tranquebar under the command of Captain Frorup; as well as two French ships, one carrying 48 cannons, the other 24.

On 2 February I went ashore there, and //8// discovered that innermost in the bay there is very good water, but it is very difficult to fetch. Ten men had to row almost 1 mile in to the watering place, while the ships are forced to stay out in the entrance to the bay. This is not for fear of shallow ground or too little room to manoeuvre – since the entire French fleet of warships could lie a comfortable ¼ mile from the innermost end of the bay. [Rather] it is because of the onshore wind which begins to blow in the course of each day, thus keeping the ships from coming under sail; and at night it is dark, and with the land wind blowing then, it would be difficult to stay clear of the eastern shore. It should also be noted that the Negroes, although they have some empty huts at the shore – which are fishermen's huts – actually have their good-sized villages a half-mile or more inland. [From these villages], with their wives and children, they bring for sale chickens, eggs, cattle, pheasants, Guinea hens, milk, palm wine, good rice, tobacco (which is not particularly good), raw cotton and, in particular, a very beautiful variety of striped cloth made of cotton yarn in all colors, spun and woven in lengths so large and long that a man could //9// easily have it made into a complete set of underwear, or a full bedspread.

One can purchase 2 cows or oxen, for slaughter, for a price of 3 iron rods, which is certainly cheap; but on further consideration, it is little enough for the money. [This is] because the traveller cannot make use of the hide, and the Blacks will not pay anything for it since they always walk around barefoot; and as for the meat itself, even though it

---

7   *Sinkesu*. To the best of my knowledge it is only the Danes, and not the Africans, who use
    this term for the red sea bream – called *sikásika/golden gold* by the latter.

looks fine and appetizing enough, probably it is so lean and unpleasant because of the many strongly-scented grasses which cover the fields, so we have only little pleasure of it.

Among all the Negroes whom I have seen along the entire coast, for some 100 miles, none are taller, better behaved, or of better build than these; but their women are much more immodest than at other places on the Guinea Coast. //**10**//

In the year **1713**, on 9 January, along with the English warship *Falmout* – on which I travelled [back] to Europe – a double sloop arrived. It was based in Barbados, but came [now] from Capo Verde or Rio Gambia, which lies a few miles below Capo Verde. It was loaded with slaves and donkeys. I saw these slaves at Esq. Robert Mohr's house in St. Michael in Barbados, along with about 200 Acra and Fida [Whyda/ Ouidah] slaves, when they were being auctioned on 2 February that same year. I heard then that a female slave from Capo Verde or Rio Gambia fetched the same price as a good Fida male slave.

Regardless of where we were on land during the journey down the entire coast, nowhere did we meet Negroes as well-armed as those on Capo Verde: since every single male, down to 10-year-old boys, had either flintlock muskets, very good French guns, or bows, or *hasagajer* – which are a spears for throwing – or canes or whips with sharp nails, or knives with the points broken.[8] [Some had] beautiful French swords; some [weapons made] of horns from the heads of swordfish, as long and wide as the *pallasker* used by cavalry when on horseback.[9] [The last mentioned] had spikes of a good inch in length on both //**11**// edges, making an extremely evil weapon.

Among the young Negroes, I saw some who went to the beach and practised throwing lances. This was done by some who took a leaf, about as large and wide as that from an apple tree, stuck the stem into the sand, and they could actually, at a distance of 12 good paces, throw their spears right through it.

When I was ashore on 2 February, as mentioned earlier, I found a poor and wretched folk. Their governor, who was also a Negro, lived

---

8   *Hasagaj* is assagai, a slender spear made of hard wood.

9   *Pallasker* are sabres with curved handles.

very poorly. I was in his hut, or house, but saw no furniture at all, apart from some reed mats on the floor on which we could lie down. He had 12 concubines there, since proper marriage, as in Christianity, is not the custom there, nor is it among any other of the Blacks. We found no fruit down at the shore, but the fields were covered with nicely scented herbs, and I myself plucked cotton from the trees, which are like our willow bushes. On the same occasion I saw the reverence shown by the Blacks for their governor, demonstrated by drumming and singing.

There, as well as everywhere else on the Negro Coast //12// , they can, on the spot, compose a song; and they deserve praise in that even when 20 or 30 sing together, they still stay in key, so that one never hears them out of tune.

The governor came out in mediocre finery, in his canoe, which is a kind of boat known as a *knubskib* or *eege* in Danish.[10] It is made of a single tree trunk that is hollowed out and formed to a point. It is higher both fore and aft, but the stern forms a flat seat, where the remidor or paddler sits and steers the boat with his paddle.[11] They do no use *pagaier*, or paddles, made in the same manner as ours; theirs are not more than 2 *alen* long, formed like our spade, yet not straight at the end but more like a pointed rhombus.[12]

Some, particularly far up the coast, use canoes that are round underneath; others are flat and the sides are vertical. At some places you can see such boats that are so large and long that one could load them with 10 or 12 iron rods, 1 *pipe* of wine or brandy, and 11 men, each with his paddle.[13] But the smallest ones hold 3 or 5 men //13//. This type of vessel is made of a very porous and light variety of wood which is very compact, yet it floats on the water like a cork. This variety of tree is very tall, of great girth, and grows as extensively [in Africa] as the largest oaks in Denmark. It bears no other fruit than a very soft wool, which is so fragile that it cannot be spun or worked. There it

---

10  *Eege/ege* is a pram, a flat-bottomed boat.

11  *Remidor* is from Portuguese *remador*, oarsman, boatman. A number of Portuguese terms were commonly in use on the Guinea Coast.

12  *Alen*, a linear measure = 0.6277 m. or approx. 2 feet.

13  *Pipe* is an old English liquid measure – used for wine only – = 126 gallons/ 572.5 litres.

is called *cappot,* and is the same tree as the one we call 'silk cotton'.[14] Dapper calls this tree *bonde.*

Using this kind of canoe the governor sat right down on the bottom, and as soon as he went ashore there were 10 men standing [at attention] with guns. They each fired a shot and he then went into his house. Shortly afterward he rode off with one of the French captains on a pitiful horse.

The horses in that country are both few in number, small and good for nothing (yet for a prince, as he is considered to be among them, the horse could not be worse than it was). [*sic*] But they showed him even greater honour: a Black knelt on the ground and the governor used his back to mount his horse. [The governor] was immediately given a lance, but before he rode off one of the Blacks fell to his knees and kissed the horse's tail.

---

14  The tree is the kapok (*Ceiba casearia*).

# Chapter Two

//**14**// On the same day I occupied myself by observing their miserable and empty houses or huts, but saw no living creature at their sea houses. I also tried their palm wine, which was not particularly good.

In the area behind the *negeri* we saw a few cows and calves, not unlike the cattle one finds in Valdres, here in Norway.[15] I also saw 2 camels, and was able to by a little milk. Towards evening I bought a pheasant for a string of glass beads worth 2 sh.

On this occasion I shall also give a brief description of that bird. The pheasants there, as well as on the Guinea Coast, are much larger than those we have in our country. They have long legs, like a young turkey, the body is much larger than that of our ordinary chickens, very short and round, tail feathers that hang down, a fine long neck, blue-grey feathers with some white specks scattered throughout. It has a bald or bare head, whose skin is bluish, except for a white flap of skin as large as a shilling at each ear. The rooster has no comb but a small strip of thick, smooth red skin on his beak, and 2 small flaps on either side of his head, like an ordinary young rooster.

//**15**// On 4 Feb. we had the vice-governor of the French castle there – called Gouré – on board our ship. He was a handsome, serious and unassuming man.

On 5th, or the next day, I was ashore at the castle and found the governor quite ill and bedridden. At that castle one can obtain very good elephant tusks, good slaves and some gold, although not of the best sort. All the goods must be brought to the castle by canoe. The French keep a tight hold over their trade, and should a stranger venture to trade with

---

15  *Negeri* can be translated as ' Negro settlement'.

merchants from that country, he is forced to pay 1,000 French guilders as punishment, as well as losing his goods. Nor do they allow any foreign ship to stay in their harbour in order to purchase water, firewood or provisions before the captain has shown his pass to the commander.

That same evening we entertained ourselves by casting fishing nets [in the waters] under the castle, and took in a superabundance of fish, both large and small. Among the fish we caught was one that had a strange appearance, unlike anything I have seen before or since. Its body and tail resembled a garfish, but the skin was //16// more dark-grey, and it was not green inside near the bones. The head and mouth were like that of an eel, but between the head and body there was a hard, green, hornlike hollow tube, nearly 1 quarter *alen* long and in circumference like an ordinary manilla cane – very clear and transparent, but quite empty.

On 6 Feb., at 10 o'clock in the morning, we sailed away from there, in the name of Jesus. We had a fairly accommodating wind and desirable weather; we saw a great many fish but did not catch any. Thus, I shall take this opportunity to describe several varieties of fish that are found along the coast of Africa.

Porpoises do not hesitate to appear when they hear a musical instrument played loudly. I noticed this on the way home, too. When our trumpet players came up on the poop and performed their services, we usually saw them, if the sea was still and calm. Then we saw them mostly at sunset, in great numbers, as they tumbled and gambolled around the ship. They are often as long and stout as a fully-grown man, and, as I found out in the city of St. Michael on Barbados, //17// where I tried eating a piece of porpoise meat, it is laced with fat and tastes like cod-liver oil. Their internal organs resemble those of a pig in every way. Sometimes you find a single offspring inside them, but no more than one, and it is as large as a half-grown coal-fish.

There are many, large, sharks to be seen there, who usually stay around the ship, where there are many people and slaves on board, since the dead bodies – which there are far too often – are their share. Ordinary men eat the shark meat at times, but with very little pleasure, because it is a very dry and tasteless fish.

There is often a variety of fish called 'suckers' that follows us. (The Dutch call it *stront visch*, because they maintain that human waste is that fish's favourite food).[16] There are no ballan wrasse or 'rock suckers' such as those caught along the Norwegian coast.[17] These fish, when they have been caught on a hook or in a net, and feel that they are being drawn up, if they are near a rock face or a stone on the bottom of the sea, fasten themselves by sucking so tightly that unless the stone is too large to be pulled up with them, they would rather let themselves by torn apart //18// than release their hold. This fish, which has red-grey scales and skin, has a round fleshy pad as large as a *daler* under its stomach.[18] It is with this it fastens itself so securely. It is a very tasty fish. But the African suckers caught there have a smooth skin and are as large as a small coal-fish, or a cod. These have, from the neck and all they way out to the thickest part of the back, a strange arrangement, or appendage, made like the long surface of the pocket scraper commonly used some time ago to scrape Brazilian tobacco. As soon as this fish feels that it has been caught on a hook (this was the only fish that would bite our hooks) it throws its back swiftly against the side of the ship and immediately sucks itself so tightly to the side that it would rather be torn apart than let go. If you put it on its back on deck it sucks itself there, too, and if you want to take hold of its head and pull it towards you, it slides along the boards. But if you want to pull it by the tail, you will pull it apart rather than be able to move it from that spot. If you want to take it by the head and tail and move it //19// it will let itself be torn in two before it lets go. The meat is particularly good and tasty.

In the months of Jan., Feb., and March there are usually, at Akra on the Gold Coast, two varieties of small fish. The first type is called sardines, which have a lot of small bones. It can be salted and is used like herring, which it closely resembles. The other variety is *aboes*, which seem to be a kind of small perch. They are better fried than cooked.

The months of April and May are the worst fishing times on that coast, when there are hardly any fish to be caught.

---

16  Dutch *stront visch* translates as 'feces fish'.

17  That variety is *Labrus bergylta*.

18  The *daler*, a large coin, was divided into 6 marks of 16 shillings each.

In the months of June, July and August there is the good *sinkesu*, which were mentioned earlier on p. 7. They are like the bream in Denmark, but the scales and skin are red, although with a lovely white meat.[19]

In the months of September and October there are mostly *korkobados*, which can provide 3 men with food sufficiently and well.[20] I know of no fish in our country to which I can compare this one.

In the months of November and December there is mostly tunny, which, without a doubt, //20// is a variety of overgrown mackerel or tuna. At times we see a variety of fish called Brazilian cod, which is of the same type and characteristic as the cod in the northern lands, that is, it is poor and inedible from April until September.

They also catch the fish called *dorado* [dolphin], which looks much better than it tastes. 3 men could easily have a full meal on a grown *dorado*. When seen in the sea at night it seems to resemble a golden log shot past the ship. We shot a few of them with a harpoon from the head of the ship, otherwise it is caught by a hook.

*Albocoro* [albacore] is a fairly large fish, but with very dry meat.[21] The best parts are the head and stomach, the rest is very dry and unpleasant.

Grey mullet are caught in the lagoons, when they have become so overfilled in the rainy season that they break through the sand bar. It is a very fat and good fish.

In the lagoon under Christiansborg one can also get some shrimp, especially in the months of September and October, but //21// a single one of them is twice as large as those we catch in Denmark.

Oysters are found here at times, but they are much larger than those from Holstein, indeed, even than those from Norway, especially during the period when the moon is waxing.

A variety of lobster is found there at times, too, which, in appearance, are somewhat different from the Norwegian variety, but taste every bit as good.

---

19  *Abramis brama.*

20  *Korkobados* may be *Selene dorsalis,* African moonfish.

21  Albacore is a large specias of tuna.

[There are] flying fish, which I have eaten in Barbados, but without much pleasure since they are a poor variety of fish. In appearance they closely resemble the previously mentioned sardines, that is, our herring, but the head is much more pointed than that of our herring. The sea must be extraordinarily full of that type of fish, and they share the fate of the herring in that the larger fish live on them. They could, however, be seen to be more fortunate than the herring since they can save themselves by flying over the water, but not much further than a stone's throw, as long as their fins are wet. They are not seen except at 24 degrees on either side of the equator.

The fishing methods of the Blacks are various. When we are under sail //22// on the Coast, we use a large fish hook, like those used when fishing for halibut or flounder. To bait the hook we use some red and white rags or cloth, and sometimes only a couple of chicken feathers. The line to which the hook is to be fastened must be as thick as that used for the plumb line. For a full fathom or more above the hook the line must be tightly wound with brass thread or steel thread, otherwise the shark will bite it off as if it were a single thread. The bait on the hook must seem strange, but the shark is unbelievably ravenous, and when the ship has great speed he rushes after the ship and the bait as if he fears it will run away from him, and he swallows the entire bait greedily. And there, in the hot climate, he has nearly the same conditions as here in Nordland as long as the dog days last, when he does not stay in the seabed. [sic]

The sardines – which the fishermen are required to have as the most convenient bait with which they catch all the other fish – cling together or form a ball, just like the small herring in Norway, [numbering] many thousands, indeed millions in the school. There they are caught either with a fine-masked net //23// like a sack, or in a seine net that is wide or large at the bottom and ends in a point at the top, to which they have fastened a line of 20 fathoms or more. The other end is in the canoe. When they see the sardines churning the surface of the water – since they cannot catch them unless the sea is very calm – the fisherman leans over the end of the canoe and knows precisely when to throw the net over the school of fish; and because of the small lead weights fastened around the opening, he can encompass many at times, at other times only a few, fish, which he quickly draws in. Those who cannot afford a net like that take a line of 20 to 30 fathoms in length, and on that line they fasten the small fishing hooks with a small space between them, at about 7 to 8 fathoms up the line. He has no bait, but a small lead weight tied to the end. He throws this line deftly more than 20 fathoms over the school of sardines. He then pulls it in quickly, and finds hanging on the hooks at times 12, at times more, at times none at all.

At times they can catch *aboes* with //**24**// a seine, but the large fish, such as sappher, korkobados, albacores, *sinkesu* and Brazilian cod are always caught by hooks, because they do not play above the surface of the water like the small fish described above, nor do they stay near land so one might set nets to catch them.[22] Rather, it is all done in deep waters a mile or more from land, and the fisherman on that coast have neither such seine nets, nor equipment, nor, indeed, the knowledge of fishing as do these here in Norway, even though the ocean there is far richer in fish than it is here, and good fishing weather is not so rare as it is here.

The turtle – of whom the females (but never the males, they say) come up on land to lay their eggs in the hot sun so the sun can hatch them. The fishermen can catch this fish [*sic*] only at night, not in the daytime, by placing themselves between the sea and them, and they know how to tip them very rapidly over onto their backs. The turtle has then been caught. They claim, which is probably true although I have never seen it, that a turtle that is fully grown can walk with 3 men on its back. When you sail along the shore, but a couple of miles from the beach, you occasionally see //**25**// turtles lying and floating on the surface of the water in order to sun themselves, but it is impossible to catch them.

Likewise you also see, floating on the surface of the water, a sort of fish that the Portuguese call *pisce de diaboli*.[23] It is as wide and large as a good-sized round table. As regards this creature, it is a ray, but the fish in itself is no source of food. The skin, however, which is very rough

---

22  I have been unable to identify *aboes*. *Sappher* could be the *Sapphine gurnard* or sea robin.

23  Devil fish: possibly a giant of the Cephaloptera, a ray.

and sharp, is readily bought by the Negroes who pay 3 pesos – which is 12 rixdaler species – for a piece, because it is absolutely large enough to cover a shield. and is considered quite rare, like the skin of a caiman.

There is also a variety of fish that grows close to the rocks, or on hard sand, and is easily caught when there is a great ebb tide. It is round as a ball on top and rather flat on the side that is toward the rock or sand. That side has a round hole in the middle. It has scales that are closely covered with round, thin, pointed spikes about an inch long. When opened one finds nothing more inside than small roe, as large as millet grain. In Mr. //**26**// John Belliforte's house – he was the vicar in the city of St. Michael in Barbados in 1713 – I ate some of that fish. When marinated in vinegar and powdered ginger it tasted fairly good. The English call it sea egg, and consider it a delicacy. But the Negroes on the Guinea Coast do not exert themselves much in its preparation. They simply put it on the embers for frying, break off the shell, and eat it. Here in Nordland they are plentiful, but people do not bother about it.[24]

Although the Negroes at many places along the coast of Guinea have an abundance of salt they use only a little of it. If their fish is very fat they skin the back, remove the backbone, sprinkle salt on it [and leave it] for a night, then smear a thick layer of red clay over it. This prevents maggots. After a few days they lay it out in the sun on the roofs, or on a flat section of ground in their yards, until it becomes dry and hard. This fish gives rise to a great stench in the *Negerier*, which the Negroes have no trouble tolerating, and they prefer to eat this fish rather than fresh.

//**27**// Since I lived here for such a long time and had contact [with the Africans] a mere 2 short miles above Nungo – and had visited the settlement myself four times – I could walk there from 6:00 to 10:00 in the morning, and from 3:00 to 7:00 in the evening I could walk back to our fortress quite comfortably. On such occasions I have been observant and have regularly asked about their fishing equipment, but I have never seen nor heard of the baskets that Dapper describes on p. 455.

---

24 This is undoubtedly a sea urchin.

I have now, somewhat expansively, reported on the fish and fishing practices here as I have myself both seen and noted them when I was in that country. This has been done for the sake of the approving reader's pleasure, so that I will not have to report, in other places, about varieties of fish that might appear here and there.

# Chapter Three

Now I shall return to recording things in chronological order.

On 20 Feb. **1709**, early in the morning, we arrived at Capo de Monte, which is a place with lovely, high headlands covered with forest; and south and north of this there is lovely flat land. //**28**// But since there was no trade to be had for us, we weighed anchor during the day watch, and sailed off in order to continue our journey. On the next day, the 21$^{st}$, at 7$^{th}$ glass in the morning watch, we had an extremely hard *travade*. A *travade* down there is what in Nordland is called a flood-tide.[25] This is a strong and unexpected rising wind, evidently in warm weather in the summer. But this *travade* did not last long, since a couple of 'hour-glasses' later it was over.

After that, on 22$^{nd}$ of the same month, towards evening, we sailed up under Capo Masurado, and anchored there. But when we realized that there was to be no trade there either, we weighed anchor again and continued along our course.

On 23$^{rd}$, at 3:00 in the afternoon, we noticed a Dutchman who was a Zeeland interloper under the same Capo.[26]

Still on the 26$^{th}$, in the evening, we anchored outside of Rio de St.

---

25  *Travade* from the Portuguese *trovoada*, sudden thrunderstorm, is now known as a line squall. The term was used variously as *travat, travado*. It is not, as Rask claims, the same as a flood-tide. A line squall is rainfall caused by the meeting of two main air masses, when the warmer one is forced to rise by the cooler one underneath it. It is characterized by a long line of black clouds, a rise in wind speed as it passes, accompanied by heavy rains, thunder and lightning. See E.A. Boateng *A Geography of Ghana*, p.32. A flood-tide, on the other hand, is an unusually high tide caused when the sun and the moon, pulling together in the same direction, are creating the tide.

26 'Interlopers' were private traders who were allowed to trade on the Guinea Coast by paying a percentage of their profits to the Company, but were in constant rivalry with the Company's own ships.

Jean, where we had good weather all night, but we left there as soon as morning broke.

On 27$^{th}$, during the day watch, we had a very hard *travade*, with thunder and lightning. During the 2$^{nd}$ glass of the day watch, we saw a sailor coming dead ahead from the east; //29// he showed a Dutch flag first, but one glass later he stood and showed a French flag. He came straight for us in the evening, and we saw then that he was the smallest of the French ships and cruisers that we had seen at Capo Verde. After the 3$^{rd}$ glass of the first watch we had a very strong *travade*, with fearsome thunder and lightning, which lasted for a couple of glasses.

On the last day of that month, the 28$^{th}$, we were under Rio Sestre at 3:00 in the afternoon, and in the evening we saw two ships north of us that were interlopers from Zeeland. We found this out the day after. When it had become dark the Frenchman weighed anchor and set out on a hunt to the south, after one of the Dutchmen. We never learned the outcome of this. The Frenchman told us – which pleased us greatly – that he had seen and talked to our countryman, the ship *Quintus*, the day before.

At the same place, on the 1 March, 5 canoes came out to us [and their crew came on board]. They had very good elephant tusks for sale, but kept the price inordinately high. This was due to the interlopers, who ruin trade nearly everywhere.

//30// On the same day, towards midday, we left there and saw the 'White Rock' at our side, at the 4$^{th}$ glass of the dog watch. This certainly shines in the eyes of those who sail past.

On the 2$^{nd}$ of the same month, at the same time – 4$^{th}$ glass of the dog watch – we had a small *travade*, accompanied by fearful thunder and lightning, and in the calm that followed we were forced to anchor.

At 9:00 on the following morning, 3$^{rd}$ March, 7 canoes boarded us with a supply of good elephant tusks and some sacks of malaget, but nothing was purchased. And I must now take the opportunity to explain the above-mentioned malaget. This does not grow on small trees, like pepper, but quite like poppies in Denmark, but with a much larger seed pod and seed, almost the size of buckwheat. The stems on which the seed pods grow are long and round, and the pods that contain the seeds – some 100 seeds in each pod – are as large in their round form as a chicken egg. Inside they are divided into 4 sections. The pod with the seeds is harvested twice a year, in February and //31// August, and when the fruit is well-dried in the sun, after a few days, the seed is taken out of the pod and kept, while the pod or shell is thrown away. Everyone buys this for their slaves; both the Blacks and the Christians use it, since proper pepper is only, and very rarely, available on the European ships arriving there, and is very expensive. It is used like pepper, and the Blacks grate it on a flat stone, like millie – which I shall describe later – and when it is very fine, they mix it with the juice of the small citrons found here, called *brambas*. They smear this on their faces when they have a headache, and on their backs when they have back pains, since it always brings some relief and comfort to the sufferer. When I am suffering from dysentery – which, alas, is far too common among the Christians in this country – I have had myself massaged with it every second hour, and have found some relief from the insufferable pain that accompanies that malady.

On the same day, in the evening, others came out in a very large canoe with some goods, some tusks, and some sacks of malaget. //32// I observed [the canoe] carefully, and was astonished at the size of the tree from which it was made. However, Dapper, on p. 475, somewhat exaggerates the thickness of the trees at Axim, etc. where he says, rightly, that the largest canoes are made. But I have been in places where I have seen many of that variety; which I have measured and ascertained that none of them exceeds 10 fathoms in girth. Otherwise, one finds the canoes at Akra on the Gold Coast not so well made, as that same Dapper records. But at St. Thoma and Anna Bona – which are two islands belonging to the Portuguese – I have seen them made just as he described them, and what is more, even with a bow and keel both fore and aft. At Akra I have also seen Portuguese Brazilian canoes made in this way, and have found that these were much more comfortable for riding in and out of the surf than are the round, or flat, Guinean types.

I am unacquainted with the reed bridges, described by Dapper p.

476, that the Negroes are said to use for crossing the lagoons. Nor have I heard of them on the Gold Coast, but I have heard that particularly those living at //**33**// Rio Volta have, instead, two or sometimes more coconut trees bound together in their full length, where one man stands upright at the back end of it, and with a long bamboo pole – that is, an overgrown manilla rod – pushes himself forward in shallow water. But if it is too deep, they paddle or row in the manner of the country.

On such [rafts of] coconut trees they cross the lagoon easily with very large cargoes, but they always get wet, obviously, from sitting on the logs themselves. This does not bother them greatly, since water, as they say in a proverb, is dry in Guinea.

But we bought none of the goods they had in the above-mentioned large canoe, since a violent *travade* rose unexpectedly and we had to rush off sea to avoid greater danger.

The following day, 4 March, we made as great speed as we could wish, but in the evening we anchored again under Grand Setre, where there were crowds of people who wanted to trade with us.

Early in the morning of the 5th we had //**34**// more than 40 canoes alongside. There we bought 10 barrels of malaget. We left at 11:00 in the morning, and shortly after sundown the same evening we had a proper *travade*, with a great deal of rain and thunder and lightning. On that same evening, at 8:00, one of our sailors died; his name was Ole Christensøn Træden.

Next day, the 6th, after prayers were said, the dead body was lowered over board just outside of Groaj. In the evening we again had a strong *travade*, with heavy rains, thunder and lightning.

We sailed on the 7th with good weather, but in the evening there came another *travade*, but not as strong as the one before.

On the 8th, towards evening, the wind fell off, and since the current was running strongly against us, we had to anchor under Tabo, where I noted that a better landing place cannot be found on the entire coast than in the Bay of Tabo. There you are spared all the breakers and heavy surf of the sea, and even the largest boat can lie close up to the hill on the west side of the bay, and load as much as the vessel can carry.

Here we were able to purchase a *lakof,* or sack, of citrons.[27] //35// The *lakofer,* or sacks, in which the Negroes usually bring their goods are made of bark from the back of the branches of the coconut trees. This is easy to pull off and be torn into narrow strips. The English take a quantity of them home and sell them to chair makers. It was in such a *lakof* that our citrons were delivered to us.

Otherwise there was no trade there, but because of a constant sea wind and the current running against us, we had to stay here for two entire days.

In the morning, during the dog watch on 22 March, when we were adrift, we discovered that the anchor line down close to the anchor was frayed, and no matter how hard we tried to set another anchor in the seabed, we drifted so far from the buoy that, at daylight, we could not find it again, neither with the sloop nor with the boat. Therefore we had to take advantage of the favourable wind that was blowing then, and sail on our way.

At midday we experienced a strange eclipse of the sun that was so extensive that the sun was nearly darkened, apart from 1/10 of its surface.

//36// After that, on 12th of the same month, right at the beginning of the dog watch, a terrific *travade* descended upon us, with dreadful rainfall, thunder and lightning.

On the following day, 13th, at midday watch, we caught sight of two ships westward of us, one at anchor and one under sail. At 3:00 in the afternoon we arrived under Kutru, [close] to a ship that lay at anchor, and found, to our pleasure, that it was the ship *Christianus Quintus,* under skipper Hans Maas, and like us, sailing for our Company, heading for Guinea. The same ship had left Copenhagen 5 weeks and a few days before we had, and, as we understood, had been as far as 64 degrees north; and did not come out of the North Sea until two months after having left The Sound. However, when we met him, he had all his people with him: no one dead or ill, all well in every way,

On the day after, the 14th, trade went very well, and at about 6:00 in the afternoon *Quintus* weighed anchor and sailed on ahead of us.

---

27   'Citron' formerly included both lemons and limes, as well as the actual fruit as we now know it.

At the end of the day watch, on the 15$^{th}$, we weighed anchor and left Kutru, since the Negroes had no //**37**// more to trade with at that place, but we anchored again 1 mile below there at Capo Lahu. There, to our surprise, we found among the Negroes individuals so highly experienced in trade that if you put weights from 6 different countries in front of them, they could immediately identify which people and from which country they came. But, and precisely because of that, there was no trade with any advantage to be had for us, and nothing for our people to do there, so we weighed anchor at midday.

A little while after the beginning of the dog watch, on the 16$^{th}$, we had a great *travade* with much thunder, lightning and rain. This is nearly a daily occurrence at this time of year, but more or less violent, of longer or shorter duration, until daylight.

Towards evening on the 17$^{th}$ of the same month, we stopped under Capo Apollonia, in the hope of some sort of trade, which did not fail us.

The day after, on the 18$^{th}$, we purchased gold and 4 slaves. I noted not the least resentment on their part, not even any physical opposition, at their being handed over to us, from which I concluded that //**38**// the slaves must truly be treated very badly by their own people, since so few show discontent at being sold. But the revolts which they instigate, at times, when they are still near land (since they would never do so at sea, because if they did gain control they would never find their way to land again), these revolts happen purely because they are afraid of the sea and the journey. In this respect I have heard of an unpleasant conception the slaves have – as interpreted to me by one of my Boys, and indeed as many slaves have – that they believe that the *Blanke*, as they usually call the Christians, buy them for one purpose, which is that when they are out to sea they will sink them to the bottom and use them to gather *bossies*. I shall explain later what *bossies* are.

In the same way, on the 19$^{th}$, we purchased 2 slaves and small lot of gold. On the same day a Dutch cruiser came up to us. It was *The African Galley*, the Captain's name was Rein; they had boarded in Amsterdam.

# Chapter Four

Finally, on the 20th March, after 1 slave and a portion of gold had been purchased, we left there at midday and sailed away. And in the afternoon we traded more while under sail, //**39**// purchasing 2 slaves and some gold. In the evening, at 6th glass in the 'dog watches', we were under the Dutch fortress, Axim.

At that place, on the 21st, we carried on a little trade, but not of much significance, since the Dutch themselves watch very carefully, and neglect nothing by which they can profit.

On the next day, the 22nd, we arrived under the Brandenborger chief fort, called Great Frideriksberg. This is very handsome, and is very well fortified. It lies on the first point of Cape Three Points, where formerly there was much good water and firewood to be had – for which reason we went there – but now the forest is diminishing by logging, and we found no water there.

I went ashore on the 23rd, at the Brandenborg fort, and, on the invitation of the Governor-General Henrik Lahme, stayed there a few days while our ship, *Friderikus Qvartus*, was being provided with firewood and water.

On the afternoon of the following day, the 24th, there came to the same road an interloper by the name of *Prinz Eugenius*, whose skipper was Peter //**40**// Dunker, a Zeelander. That same evening, close to 10:00, the General received a letter ashore saying that his successor, by the name of Franciskus De Lange – a man of 55 years of age, according to his own information, whose home was in Emden, and a man of honourable and enjoyable demeanour – had arrived, whereupon the General arranged a reception at the fortress to welcome him.

Things were then lively on the morning of the 25th, when a large canoe with 10 remidors, 1 trumpeter, and assistants from the fortress brought him in to land. As soon as he stepped ashore, I and our merchant, Mr. Peder Todberg, received him, wished him luck upon his arrival, and accompanied him up to the fort. Outside the gate stood his predecessor who received him with 8 black servants behind him.

And here I cannot refrain from reminding my readers that it is no small burden and cost that a Christian, or European, has to bear, with the many useless Boys to clothe and support. Indeed, even the poorest White must keep a Boy, even if he himself //**41**// could manage all his needs and never require help of another. If not, he is looked upon with disdain by the Blacks, who have such great bravery and sensitivity that I dare say a Negro in his straw hat and the poor covering of his nakedness is more arrogant than is the greatest European monarch in all his royal finery. It follows that a general or chief, in order to preserve his reputation, must keep 8 to 12 Boys at least; what with the food, clothing, as well as all the ornamentation with which he must decorate them for his own honour, all this costs him a great deal. But it is the custom of the land, which must be respected.

But to return to the pomp with which the new general was received. All the soldiers and company slaves stood at attention. As soon as he had come into the fort all the cannons were loaded, and the interloper, that had sent off 15 salutes when Mr. Lange left the ship, replied with 7 salutes, and each of our Danish ships with 9.

On the day after, the 16 March, Mr. Lange was handed over the full command by Mr. Lahme; his instructions were read along with //**42**// the Articles, whereupon everyone at the fort took an oath, and the ceremony ended with the sound of trumpets and the shooting of hand guns and all the cannons around the entire fort. Thus the ceremony had come to an end. On the same day, towards evening, there came to that road 2 English ships, captained by Mr. Prinz and Mr. Gordin.

On the 27th I spoke to Mr. Gordin, and since he was going to London, I sent a letter with him – in the envelopes of Messrs. Begersløv and Kok – to my family in Denmark.

On the 28th I wrote again to my home, using the envelopes of the Hon. Messrs. the Directors, [to be sent] with Mr. Lahme. In the evening of the same day a Dutch cruiser sailed by us, the same one that had met us at Cape Appolonia. He had intercepted an interloper whom he took with him to St. Georg Del Mina, which is the Dutch chief castle on the Coast.

On the 29th 2 ships set sail from Capo Tres Puntas; having arrived there two days earlier. One left for Barbados, the other went down the coast again.

On Easter Day, which was the 31st, toward the end of the day watch, we had a strong *travade* //43//. We weighed anchor immediately in order to reach Axim, where we could get firewood and water, since we had not been able, without too much expense and waste of time, to get as much as we needed from Brandenborg Fort. We set our course for Axim that same evening, yet the ship *Qvintus* sailed behind us, in order to go below [i.e. eastward of] it for the water and firewood they needed.

On the following day, 21 April, I went ashore to the Dutch fort at Axim. The fort is very solid, both by nature [?location] and construction. What we found there, which particularly deserves to be mentioned, was that we noticed an especially great show of respect and obedience on the part of the Negroes towards the Christians, more so than at the other places. This is so because the Chief Commissioner, Mr.Lautman, practises strict discipline over everything, which the Negroes absolutely are in need of, since they are depraved creatures, who in no way can have too much restraint, which Mr. Lautman administers righteously. At the same place there is much pure gold to be had, whose better can scarcely be found at any other place. Here I relaxed and enjoyed myself for several days.

//44// On Thursday, the 4th, I went on board again and found that our people, and especially our newly purchased Negroes, were occupied with loading water and firewood.

On the 7th I was ashore again, and after a meal with Assistant Commissioner Mr. Hermans and Merchant Mr. Todberg, I went to the Dutch lodge Ankoper [Ankobra], that lies a short mile above Axim. This lodge has been well fortified by nature. It lies on a very high hill to which a path has been cleared that is wide enough for 3 men abreast. West of the lodge, ¼ mile, there is a river called Ankoper, of which, although it has been followed for a full 8 days, no end has been found. The conclusion, as rumour has it, is that it flows more than 100 miles into the interior.

On the 8th I went aboard again, with the merchant, since all the wood and water needed had been loaded, and everything was ready [for departure].

Thereupon, at 9 o'clock in the morning of the 9th, we were under sail again. But we had to anchor again at noon because of increasingly calm weather. At about 3 o'clock in the afternoon we had a small gale, weighed anchor again, and sailed thus //45// slowly down [the coast]. Towards evening we had to stop again for fear we would come too close to land with the approaching calm.

Shortly after the beginning of the dog watch, on 10 April, weighed anchor with a rising land wind, and on the same day, at 10 o'clock in the morning, our captain received a letter from Mr. Maas, who was sailing the ship *Qvintus* that lay at Dichesk [Dixcove], an English fort, containing the news that on the 7th of that month, at night, an assistant named Knud Hammer, from Norway – a very well-behaved and upright young man of good family – due to the sudden rolling of the ship, had fallen overboard from the ship's awning, where, in a moment of imprudence, he had lain down to sleep. On that day we sailed past Great Frideriksberg, Takelma and Akoda, that belong to the Brandenbergers, and, towards evening and the approaching calm, had to anchor above Dikesko.

On the morning of the 11th we weighed anchor with a small gale from the land wind that, by a few glasses into the midday watch, carried us down to Butru, a small Dutch fort, where we anchored; and in the evening our merchant was carried into land to order millie, which, of necessity, was purchased there.

//46// On the day after, the 12th, I went ashore there, too. I visited the fort, which is just a small one, on a high sandy hill, but nicely constructed; the approach is just a short, narrow path. Under the hill, on the south side, flows a very pretty river, originating, I am told, a good 12 miles up country. Some 8 or 10 months ago the Dutch began to establish a sugar plantation 1½ miles above the fort. This is beginning to yield a generous harvest already, and expectations are high for future gains from that plantation, due to the good location on flat land, with fresh water and extensive forest. Around the forest grow bitter orange trees in great numbers and with large quantities of fruit. I saw a tamarind tree there that has not yet begun to bear fruit, but the earth there yields millie in great quantities. Thus the Dutch have already, for a couple of years, been sowing robust millie seed and will certainly have enough to provide their company ships.

At the beginning of the day-watch on the 13th, we weighed anchor again, and with a good, steady, wind were able to anchor in the evening at //47// Great and Small Commendo, of which one belongs to the English and the other to the Dutch. On the following day, the 14th, we weighed anchor during the day watch, in order to come closer to land, and anchored again at 8 bells in the morning, at 7 fathoms. We had a try at trade here, purchasing 7 slaves and, of necessity, palm oil. This is called Guinean butter because, although it does not taste very good – especially before one has become accustomed to it – one must use it instead of butter, which is too dear for the ordinary person at these places. But it may, in truth, be called the most excellent medical agent in the country. The Negroes smear it over their entire bodies daily, although when they can get it, they also use old, rank tallow that is brought from Europe in small casks – but palm oil is the best; and because of that their bodies stay flexible and supple until an advanced age. When it comes to bruises, scratches, blows, or cuts, as well as sores caused by the so-called 'worm' – from which boils break on many [persons], especially on the fleshy parts of the body, and cause //48// great pain – nothing is better than a salve of palm oil. And when you become accustomed to eating it, it keeps your stomach in a very good and healthy condition; so we can reasonably consider it a great gift from God.

# Chapter Five

On the second day after this, the 16<sup>th</sup>, we weighed anchor at the end of the day-watch, and at midday we arrived at St. Jago and St. George Del Mina, 2 fortresses that belong to the Dutch. The first one, situated on a high hill, is very well fortified and is the key to the latter, which is very strong, more due to its construction than to nature. This is the chief fort of the Dutch and is of great significance. There is a *negeri* under it, which, when the Governor-General – Mr. Wesell at present – is in command, can easily muster more than 3,000 well-armed men in the space of 2 or 3 hours.

In the road here we found Captain Bording – of whom we have spoken before – with the interloper he had seized, as well as a Dutch slave ship which had been away from home for 11 months. This ship brought the Dutch African Company //**49**// only poor profit: it had sailed easily and well enough over the sea, but when it came into the tradewinds – which we must constantly be aware of, their being some 30 degrees north of the equator – it had not paid attention to their log readings, so that instead of coming in to Del Mina, they landed at Fida, about 80 miles below [to the east]; whereupon the first mate, for fear of being accused and seriously punished for his carelessness, and for having caused damage to the Company, went and hanged himself.[28] The captain did his best and arrived at Del Mina after several months, since sailing from Fida and up to Del Mina with a ship is evidently very difficult to achieve. [This is because] one has to sail down under the

---

28  Judging longitude was a constant problem for ships at that time; indeed until the design and perfection of maritime time-keepers, chronometers, were accepted and brought into use in the late eighteenth and early nineteenth centuries. For that story, see Dava Sobel *Longitude*, 1995; William J.H.Andrewes, ed. *The Quest for Longitude* 1996.

equator first, at times a good couple of degrees or more to the south, before coming up to 10 or 12 degrees north towards the tradewinds. Otherwise the goal cannot be achieved, especially with such a poorly navigable ship, as that one appeared to be. But when the captain arrived at Del Mina, after much difficulty, he was ordered //**50**// to sail back home to the fatherland, under arrest.

On 18th April I went ashore there and, to my great pleasure, saw the fortress and how well appointed it was. One must be particularly impressed with the excellent choice of cannons, made of pure, costly metal. This is proof of the Dutch wisdom, because it is well known that although gun-metal cannons cost much more than iron, yet iron – especially in those lands – rusts very quickly. So one must admit that it was wise to invest in the greater cost at first, than to tolerate the damage that would come later, since 1 gun-metal cannon lasts longer than 10 made of iron; and if they should have to be used in serious shooting, for which they would always have to be prepared, it is obvious how long iron cannons can be used in such a hot climate.

Nothing is lacking at the fortress, everything that you could wish for is available in the best condition. They are supplied with a smithy, a slave yard and 2 very fine underground //**51**// cisterns made of clinkers [*i.e.*tiles], which easily hold 2000 barrels of water that is healthy and tasty. It would be too complicated to describe in detail every single thing found in the fortress – things chosen with excellent taste, at great cost, and installed most conveniently. Outside the fortress there is a shady path, of about 200 paces, that leads down to the garden, which is about one-half mile in circumference, and contains many herbs, plants and trees, some of which I shall describe now with great pleasure, and for my readers' enjoyment, just as I myself saw them.

To begin with I shall treat of the pineapple, the most tasty fruit that I have ever eaten. It grows nearly like an artichoke, on a strong straight vertical stem, on the top of which sits the chief fruit, which is the largest, in comparison to the fruits that can be seen to crop out on the sides of the main stem. There are often 2 – at times, but rarely, 3 – on that stem, but those who love and cultivate this fruit do not allow more than one to grow, so that it can be better, larger and //**52**// more beautiful. Those fruits that are found growing on the sides of the stem are called 'pineapple's children' by the Negroes. When the pineapple is fully ripe it usually turns yellow one side. Then they cut it off without delay so that the crown that is at the top of the stem will not grow further and draw all the juice from the fruit, since the heat naturally drives the plant to increase in height. The fruit itself is oblong, round and thickest at the bottom; and around the entire shell, or skin, there are small pointed spikes. When you want to eat it you peel off the skin quite thickly, including the spikes, cut the fruit into slices which have a fairly large [firm] section in the center of the fruit. The slices can be immersed in clean water, or, even better, in claret, and left there for about an hour. Then it can be eaten with great pleasure, since the fruit itself has a scent like the best garden strawberries, and they seem to melt in your mouth, in the most superlative juices. The wine in which the slices had been places – especially if it is claret or any other not too strong wine – retains an especially pleasant //53// scent, like muscatel wine. A strong wine in which the fruit has been soaked can no longer be used for drinking since the fruit itself is very strong.

It has very large, long leaves – the longest and widest of them being a good five quarters of an *alen* in size – a width that the Negroes know how to use very cleverly. First they dry them well, then they pound them, crush them, and draw the fibres out of the leaves. These are then twisted dextrously, thread by thread, over their bare thighs. Although these fibres cannot easily be spun on a spinning wheel, they can easily be twisted to the desired length. Truly, I believe, that the pineapple could be worked even better, if it came into more expert hands.[29]

The English call this fruit 'pineapple', undoubtedly because no other fruit resembles it: not because of colour, but only because of its outward appearance, like those so well-known pine cones in Norway, although pineapples are much larger, as one can surmise from the foregoing description.

//54// Next I shall tell about *patatas* [sweet potatoes], which fruit [*i.e.* edible part] is purely the roots. These *patatas* are a variety

---

29  For use of pineapple leaf fibre – for nets and suitable for textiles – see Isert (1788/1992) 142; *idem* (2007) 189-90..

of root that grows in clusters underground in very large quantities. It shows only the leaves above the ground. The roots are a little longer and somewhat thicker than our potatoes and are said to be good to eat, if you know how to prepare them properly and have available what is needed for that preparation. They are cooked at sea, and placed on salt meat, as we in Norway do with turnips. But on the English islands in America large quantities of *patatas* are cut into pieces and placed in lukewarm water, covered, for 3 days. Then both the fruit and the water are cooked together in a large kettle. The impurities that collect are skimmed off constantly, and when they feel that it has cooked long enough they leave it to cool. Then it is bottled and tightly bound, and they use it to drink, in their houses, like their daily beer. They call it *mabier*: it has a slightly sour taste and is //**55**// delicious, but is not considered very healthy to drink.

I shall combine *pisang* [plantain] and *bakkoves* [bananas] because they seem, by appearance, to be a variety of [the same] tree, since, when they are full-grown the trunk is 10 to 12 feet high. It is a very loose and poor type of tree, out of whose crown the branches seem to spring and spread out of its own husk, until, because of their own weight, they finally bend over on all sides. Under these hanging branches, yet as if out of the opening at the very top of the stem, the fruit hangs in clusters and bunches of 10 to 12 of the former, 12 to 16 of the latter variety. In length, a *pisang* can be more than a quarter of an alen long, four-sided, and as thick as an ox horn. But the *bakkoves* is neither as long or as thick, yet it is that fruit that is much more pleasant and tasty than the first one. There is a noticeable difference between the leaves, since the leaves of the *bakkoves* are about 7 quarters of an *alen* in length and 1 quarter in width, while the leaves of the *pisang* tree are as long as a grown man, //**56**// and roughly one-half *alen* in width. And it seems reasonable that our first parents, who after their Original Sin found themselves naked, covered themselves with fig leaves – as it is translated in *Gen*:3. v:7 – may have found that the leaves of this kind of tree that could suffice as cover; and this same idea is reinforced by many, which can be seen in Gabr: Sionita Libr: *De Urbib: & Morib: Orient*: p. 55. Also in Joh. Henr. Horringher; *Histor. Orient.* Libr. I chapter 3, p. 117; Job. Ludolf: *Histor. Æthiop.* Libr I. Ch. 9, sect. 21, and others.[30] Truly, in all of nature there is not to be found a leaf that could be more suitable for this purpose. Also, in Syria, in Damascus, many of this variety of tree grow; and the inhabitants at those places commonly have the same opinion, calling the fruit 'Adam's apples' and the tree *mautza* or *almautz*.[31]

On this occasion I must write about the coconut tree. It grows up to an impressive height and, in the same way [as the *pisang* and *bakkoves*], has all its branches and leaves growing out of the top of the trunk. Closely under the branches hang //57// the coconuts, very close together, but not in clusters like the *pisang* or *bakkoves*, for each coconut has its own stem.

The wild coconut trees are in every way similar in appearance, and bear their fruit in the same way and at the same places [on the trunk], but they are good for nothing since there are neither kernels nor anything useful in the nuts. I have never seen so many of the good coconut trees growing in groves as they do at Axim and Capo Tres Puntas. When I was there I wanted to know the real reason for their planting so many of that kind of tree; whereupon the Negroes, with the help of an interpreter, answered that they do this purposely so that they can then tell how old their children were. Otherwise, no one knows how old he is, nor do they bother much about it. I continued to ask – standing next to a young tree – how old one of his children was – who was close by and for whom the tree had been planted; to

30  Gabriel Sionita (1577-1648), a Maronite, versed in many languages. He is famous for his share in the publication of the Bible, in Paris, in a number of languages- He also published *Geographia Nubiensis*, to which there was an appendix treating of life and customs in the Orient – the area covering largely what we consider today to be the Middle and Near East. Hiob Ludolf (1624-1704),.a German orientalist, was the founder of the study of Ethiopian language and literature in Europe. He published an Ethiopian grammar and an Ethiopian-Latin dictionary, as well as *Historia Aethiopica*, published in Frankfurt in 1681. I have been unable to identify Joh. Henr. Horringher *Histor. Orient.*

31  Actually, the banana, *Musa sapientum*, and the plantain, *Musa paradisiaca* are not trees. As for the 'fig', from about the mid-16th century and all through the 17th, Europeans often referred to bananas or plantains as Indian figs, a term they got from the Portuguese *figo da India*. Rask seems to have been confused by that. The Arabic *mawzah* for banana gives us the family name Musaceae and the genus name Musa for bananas and plantains. (I am indebted to Stanley Alpern for this information.)

which the interpreter answered – after the Negro's reply – '5 years', and he counted five joints from the root up to the crown, and part of the sixth. From this I learned – which I have since noted – //**58**// that that kind of tree sets one joint every year, but as it ages the joints become shorter, yet are still clearly visible both on the bark and inside the trunk itself. But it does not grow more than 25 or, at the most, 30 years, since I do not recall seeing any that had more than that many joints, and concluded thus, from observation, that such trees had visibly poorer and smaller fruits than the young trees, and that the tree, at about that age, begins to wither and weakens from year to year, until it dies. On a middle-aged tree there are 20 nuts, sufficient fruit for a year [*sic*].

The fruits are very large nuts that are extremely useful and good. Sometimes you find one that yields a *pegel* of very sweet juice, like milk.[32] The juice is white, like whey, but if any of it comes into contact with cotton cloth it leaves an ugly black stain that is impossible to remove. You can also write with it, although the script is not visible before it is held over a fire to dry. Besides this juice there is a large, firm, sweet kernel that sits //**59**// right inside the shell, in a way like a mother, in whom the milk is found.

The so-called *uranie-apple* [bitter orange?] trees and citron trees are found, in great numbers of both varieties in the garden, and I shall not write about the many edible herbs so well-known in Europe, that are also available there in great quantities.

Now I must move out of the garden and go outside of the fortress, to report on some of the things I noticed there. Around the fortress and the *Negeri*, on the west side, there is a river that runs out into the sea.[33] It is so wide and deep that a good-sized Portuguese ship lay there at the quay. Although the mouth of the river is not very deep, further up-river there are many places that are 2 or 3 fathoms deep. In short, everything there is well worth seeing.

The *Negeri*, which has many thousand *caser,* or houses, that are all built with walls of grey stone, and on all the streets and alleys there

---

32  Pegel = ¼ *potte,* or 0.242 litre.

33  Pra River.

is an abundance of all kinds of food available for sale.[34] At the end of the *Negeri* lies an old Portuguese chapel, where there is a guard every night; and around the walls of the chapel, on both sides, there is a thick ring-wall with //**60**// numerous arrow loops, stretching from the fresh-water river and across to the sea, [so that?] no one from the mainland would be able to attack the *Negeri*.

After that, on 10 April, during the day watch, we sailed away from there, and anchored again, at 9 bells in the morning, at Cape Coast, which is the headquarters of the English, and is as well-fortified and equipped as Del Mina. A small cannon shot east of this is Frideriksberg, which, in earlier times, was the chief fort of the Danes; but in Governor Hans Lyke's time the Danes lost it, and it is now called 'Danish Hill'. It lies so conveniently on a hill that one could easily shoot at Cape Coast from there, and is therefore, now, like a key for the larger [fort].

The day after, the 20th, I was at the fortress Cape Coast, and found everything there in a very proper condition. At dinner I had the honour of dining with the Director-General, My Lord Thomas Dalby. [We dined] in the garden, which, in circumference, cannot be much less than a mile. All the paths are lined with citron, bitter orange and orange trees on both sides. Not only were there Guinean, the country's //**61**// own, fruits, growing in abundance and in every variety, but there were also costly edible herbs of every kind, such as those we need and use in our country; green and white cabbage, and anything European cuisine might require. And I noticed here, as in other places in this country, that among the European vegetables which are foreign to these parts and seldom seen, wild mangold, beans, green and white cabbage, parsley, radishes, lettuce, tarragon, cauliflower, thyme, rosemary and purslane grow best in Guinea, while sugar peas, cucumbers, parsnips grow poorly.

On the Guinea coast you also find very good watermelons, sometimes as large as the largest squash. They taste really delicious, and are wonderfully refreshing, but you must take care not to drink too much water afterward, because then you would overdo, and chill your stomach , which, in this climate, is usually weak enough already.

---

34 *Caser/casa*, clearly from the Portuguese 'house'.

Particularly on the island Anna Bona, more than at other places, there are beautiful pumpkins, but on the English //**62**// islands in America you find them in greater quantities, and they use them with their food as we do root fruits.[35]

But, to return to the garden at Cape Coast. There I saw more than 100 newly planted tamarind trees. I also noticed a kind of tasty African bean growing on trees that are not higher than man. Their leaves resemble those of the willow trees in Denmark. But there were also a great number of indigo bushes, which I must write about now.

On the indigo bushes there are pods in which the seeds lie in what look like small bays. The seed falls out of itself when it is ripe, thus sowing itself. But the branches and leaves – as I have been told – are cut off during certain times of the year, placed in water and kept there until they are rotten. The rotting mass is then taken out and pressed, until the juice that has been extracted forms a thick sediment. After the water has been slowly poured off this must be dried in the sun; thus the indigo is prepared, with much labour and care.

There is no more room here for me to dwell in greater detail //**63**// on descriptions of the garden. The General himself, who is a gentlemen of 69 years, was carried to and from the garden in an upholstered chair, by 2 Negroes. There was constantly music throughout the dinner. 2 played trumpets,1 played drums, and around the room there were 8 Negroes who blew – in their way – on horns made of small elephant tusks. He had, for his personal use, 16 black servants; besides chamber servants, a cook, one to set the table and serve. And he served a very elegant meal.

On the following day, the 21st, in the morning, we weighed anchor, but dropped anchor again at midday, a little way below Cormantin, a Dutch fortress lying below Anemabu – which now belongs to the English but was formerly Danish. And Moure, a Dutch fort where the Portuguese, formerly, when they were masters of the Coast, had their headquarters.

---

35 *Anna Bona*/Annabón in Equatorial Guinea.

# Chapter Six

We weighed anchor again on the 22nd, and set the anchor in the evening a half mile above Appam, a small Dutch fort lying about a half mile above Dyvelsberg.[36] We had to stay there //**64**// the following day because we had bad weather, including *travader*, largely at night between the hours of 23 and 24, when a fearful rain, thunder and lightning overwhelmed us. This occurs much more violently and unexpectedly here than in our European countries.

Finally, on 25 April, during the dog-watch, we left that place, with Dyvelsberg on the side [*sic*] at 9 o'clock in the morning, and 2 hours later, at 11:00 in the morning, we were alongside Vimba [Winnebah], an English fort. At about 1:00 in the afternoon we had sailed in to Breku, a small, but very pretty Dutch fort.[37] Here you find fort after fort belonging to the Europeans. On that same evening we arrived safe and sound at Christiansborg – God be blessed and praised! – after having, for nearly 5 months, from 5 December 1708, seen the wonderful creations of the Lord and profited by His guidance and protection.

Now we all had plenty to do in getting our things in order after the long journey, and since my predecessor in the post was still in service, I had the opportunity of looking around and //**65**// refreshing my mind. Thus, on 27 April I was at the Dutch fort, Crevecoeur, as well as at the English fort, St. James.[38] Both are fine, small forts, lying only a short way from ours.

---

36  The Dutch fort at Apam was *Leysaemheyt (Patience)*. (van Dantzig 1980, xi, 23).

37  The Dutch fort at Breku [Senya Beraku] was *De Goede Hoop (Good Hope)*. It was built in 1702 so was very new when Rask saw it in 1709. See *ibid*. xi. 35.

38  The Dutch Fort Crèvecoeur was in 'Dutch Accra'. It was renamed Ussher Fort when taken over by the English in 1868. The English James Fort is in 'English Accra', or James-town.

After that I was given all the necessary information by my predecessor, Mr. Anders Vinter, concerning a description of the state of the office, as well as the particulars of each and every member of the congregation. On 5 May, the fifth Sunday after Easter, he took his leave of the congregation.

On 9 May, which was the Feast of the Ascension, I held my first service for the congregation for which I was now responsible. Lord! He who rose to heaven and who sits by God's right hand, and worked with His servants who went out into the world to preach the Word, He also aided me greatly in my weakness, to the honour of His Name.

On the 17th of the same month I wrote home to my family in Denmark, sending the letter with Mr. Hans Maas, Captain of the ship *Christianus Qvintus,* to let them know that, with God's help, I had now arrived at my destination, and that they could join me in praising God.

//66// On Whitsunday, which was 20 May, our second assistant, Knud Eriksøn, died in an extremely moving and devout manner. He was born in the northernmost part of the world, in Trondheim in Norway, and his death greatly moved me and all those present. His funeral was held on 21 May, at 12:00, since the deceased cannot be preserved long in that land because of the heat, and because it is the burial custom of the country.

Four days later, 25 May, the ship *Christianus Qvintus,* sailed from Fort Christiansborg to Fida, and my predecessor in this office, Mr. Anders Vinter, left on that ship on his way back to the Fatherland, exactly four years and one day after he had arrived.

On the 31st of the same month we killed a snake in our warehouse. It was more than one fathom long, and as thick as a man's arm. Such snakes, and those even larger, are very numerous and cause great damage. But on that same night there was another kind of dangerous animal in the Dutch *negeri* under Crevecoeur. There were 2 tigers, who had //67// broken into a *casa,* or hut.[39] One of them pulled a woman out of her bed, and no one ever saw, or heard of her, again. The other one grabbed hold of another woman and tore a great chunk out of her

---

39  Tigers are not found in Africa. The term was used universally by the early authors to describe all large felines.

thigh, because of which she died shortly afterward. These animals are extraordinarily greedy, especially for people, but are also indescribably clever at entering and leaving the huts, so the people must constantly be on guard against them. The other woman would certainly have been dragged off, too, had she not screamed so that many people came to [help] her, so the beast had to be satisfied with a piece of her thigh, and had run off.

Just as wild animals cause great discomfort in the country, on one hand, so do storms give rise to great fear, of which we, in a short period, had double proof. On 13 June, in the evening, we had the strongest *travade* I had experienced up to that day.

On the 16th of the same month, the 3rd Sunday after Trinity Sunday, in the morning, we had the most fearful, but at the same time the most remarkable, thunder, which – for the sake of research in natural science – I shall describe //68// as I experienced it. At 7:30 there was a great clap of thunder, but just before the actual clap was heard, there was a sound like a 4-pound cannon being fired with live ammunition, since all of us present heard it sounding like a ball whistling through the air. A short time after that there was a powerful clap and then we heard, before the clap itself, something like 3 different shots, sounding louder than those of an 18-pounder, but heard no whistling, as before. And just as the scriptures call thunder the voice of God (*Psalms* 18.14), so should we honour that voice, even in the realm of nature, to the glory of the Creator.[40]

The thunder and lightning are extremely violent, especially in the rainy season, [so violent] that nothing less than high buildings or half-timbered houses can survive them; [other types] are soon blown down.

Up to now the ship on which I came has been here under the fort, partly for unloading, partly to repair damages from the sea journey, but also to seek trade. But on 28 June, at about 12:00 midday, the ship, *Fridericus Qvartus*, weighed anchor and sailed //69// from here, in order to go farther along the coast where they might succeed in trading for some slaves, since our fort was only poorly supplied for that trade:

---

40  The reference is to Psalm 18.13 in the King James Bible.

it was the *rosar* time – or harvest time – for the Blacks, so they all had need of their slaves and no one wanted to sell any.[41]

At the beginning of the month of July, precisely on the 1st, we received the news here at the fort that the French [ship] *Du Prez* had seized a certain Dutch cruiser that had a considerable amount of gold and elephant tusks on board, so it was a truly rich, golden catch.

In contrast, the ship *Friderikus Qvartus* had nowhere near such fortune, since on 14 June it came back here to Christiansborg, having had little or no success in trade, largely because of the aforementioned conditions.

On the 19th of the same month our Governor, Lieutenant Captain Erik Lygaard, received a letter from Del Mina informing that Mr. Schonheid, formerly Chief Commissioner at Moure, had been installed, by the Dutch Guinean and West-Indian Company, as Governor-General //**70**// over all their forts on the Coast.

Not long after that, on 27 July, we received truly sad news from Fida about the ship *Christianus Qvintus*, that had sailed from Christiansborg on 25 May, with the Captain Mr. Hans Maas, Mr. Anders Vinter – the vicar who was my predecessor – and the merchant Msr. Peder Todberg aboard. We heard that they had gone ashore while the ship lay at anchor at Popo. This was on 14 June, towards evening. And when they left to go aboard again, a great wave in the breakers broke over the canoe so that it was completely flooded; and immediately after that another wave came and overturned the canoe. Merchant Todberg was immediately washed overboard so they never saw him again. Mr. Anders Vinter managed to climb up on the wreck and sit there for a short time, but a strong current came and washed him off, dragging him to the bottom immediately. Captain Maas was saved by the *remidors* and was brought ashore with a little life left in him, but no matter how much they rolled him about and did their best to revive him, he died an hour later.

//**71**// This saddened us deeply, and I could not but wonder at the great God's government, which must also be seen in all this. The ship *Fridericus Qvartus* had, on its journey out, a great loss of people, as mentioned before, but *Christianus Qvintus* had previously not lost a

---

41   *Rosar* from the Portuguese *roçar*, to plant.

single man – yet now, on its return journey, its loss was great.

The ship, *Fridericus Qvartus*, is still anchored here under the Fortress, of [whose crew] a sailor died very suddenly on 28 July, just as he was going ashore. His name was Ole Hallands Farer. Likewise, a few days later, another one died, whose name was Niels Jensøn.

The *Fridericus Qvartus* left here in the following month, August, and we heard nothing of her before 18 Sept., when we learned that everything was proceding as wished in terms of the slave trade; that they had acquired a considerable number, and all was well on board. With the same messenger we received the additional information about the other ship, *Christianus Qvintus*, which was still at Fida, that the man who became captain after Mr. Maas – a man by the name of Just //72// van der Fendevogel – was dead, after a short-lived command. He died on 5 August.

After a short time, on 4 October, a Dutch interloper appeared in the road at Christiansborg. The name of the Captain was Peter Duncher, commanding the ship *Prinz Eugenius* – which has been mentioned earlier – and who could not desist from telling us repeatedly what a difficult summer they had had, because of the pursuit by a French cruiser, but they had, up to now, managed to avoid them.

On that same evening, between 5:00 and 6:00, I unexpectedly saw the Negroes' fetish, or worship of the sea, which had, for 5 days' time, been extremely rough and so stormy that no one could go out to fish. Therefore, they performed this heathenish custom, which took place in the following way. Their *fetissiero*, who is supposed to be their kind of priest, was in charge of this affair, along with 3 *remidors* – who are those knowledgeable about canoeing and about fishing – [all] went down to the beach with a bottle of brandy.[42] They poured some into a small calabash (which is a kind of bowl made of the lowest shell of a squash) in the following way. First they remove the meat, and then dry //73// the shell in the sun. They have great numbers of these, as we, in our country, have wooden bowls, both large and small, for daily household

---

42  *Fetissiero* from the Portuguese *feitiço* meaning something constructed. The English term, also *fetish*, was used by the Europeans to describe anything and everything related to religious practices and beliefs in West Africa.

use. Some hold a half *pott* some a whole *pott* and more, some hold a half *anker* and more.[43] To continue: while holding the calabash of wine in his hand he made a speech, or prayer, to the sea, asking it to become calm; and with much bowing and scraping he drank a toast to the sea from [the calabash]. Thereafter, he poured a small amount into the sea 4 times, ordering the others to do the same, which they did. Then they all said a sort of prayer and made a farewell speech to the sea, and went up to their *caser* or huts, where all the *remidors* gathered, and, with drink, song, hornblowing, and shooting – in their manner – they celebrated, or *bringarede* as they call it, until far into the night.[44] But time would tell, subsequently, that all their services were folly since the sea did not become calm, just as giving it brandy does not seem to be the best method of calming it, as it usually makes quiet [people] restless.

On the 18th of the same month we received a letter //74// from Qvita, sent the 7th, reporting that the ship *Frider. Qvartus* had left for the West Indies on 2 October, with 434 slaves on board, of whom 49 died, but the ship *Christian. Qvintus* had left Fida a few days earlier.

On the 24th, during day watch, one of the soldiers, by the name of Michel Spormager, who was then on watch on the battery, heard a long, drawn-out scream from the ground under the hill in which the Fortress Christiansborg is located. This scream sounded to him as if it had come from a small pig. Later in the morning, after he had been relieved [of his watch], he went down behind the fortress to see if he could find any sign of the animal who had screamed so. What he found, to his great surprise, near a snake pit (of which there are many, and fearfully large, ones) was an overgrown rat, whose tail was absolutely more than an *alen* long. But what most surprised him and all the others who saw this, was that the tail was half black and half white, which everyone who knew about these things said they had never seen before. We concluded, then, that this must have been the same rat that had screamed when the snake had attacked it.

//75// In the following month, on 2 November, our Chief

---

43  *Pott/potte* = 0.968 litre; *anker* = usually 40 *potter*.

44  *Bringar* from the Portuguese *brincár*, to jest, sport, play.

Assistant, Mr. Knud Røst, came back from Qvita, and reported that on the night between 14 and 15 September a number of slaves on the ship *Frid. Qvartus* had been able to break their chains into pieces and free themselves. They intended to overrun the ship, shouted to each other everywhere, and released a number equal to those who had broken loose, planning to overwhelm the ship's crew, who had to fight with all their might to hold them off. [The outcome was that] 2 of the ship's crew were seriously injured by these desperate people, but they were, God be praised, brought under control after a hard struggle. Had that not been the case, they would have taken the life of every Christian – their loudly shouted intention – as well as having caused irreparable damage to the Company. After that, immediately on the following morning, following the decision of the entire ship's council, an execution was held. The leader of the revolt first had his right hand cut off by the bosun, and the severed hand was shown to all the other slaves, along with the serious threat that the rebellious slaves should see that this applied to all of them; after which the left hand, and then the head, were cut off. Then //76// the dead body was hoisted up under the main yard, where it hung well in sight of the slaves for 2 days. The other slaves who had taken part in the revolt were whipped, and ground malaget [pepper], salt and ashes were rubbed over their entire bodies. Thus ended a very dangerous affair.

# Chapter Seven

After that, on 24 December, one of our assistants, Niels Hansøn, came back to the fortress from Fida, where he had sailed on 25 May that same year, on the ship *Christian. Qvintus*. He reported that the slave trade was absolutely ruined there because of the great crowding of all sorts of people and ships from many countries. The French and Portuguese, who came very frequently from Brazil, were paying 3 *benda* or 96 rixdaler for a good male slave during the time when he left there.[45] Formerly one could get a good male slave for 9 pesos, or 36 rixdaler species. The reason for this great gathering of so many ships at one place is the war in Europe. Thus neither the Dutch, English, European or Brazilian Portuguese, nor any of the ships belonging to other [countries] involved in the war, would be safe from attack from one another all along //77// the entire coast above [Fida]. But all those who sail along the Coast have come to an agreement, that, at Fida, the one enemy will not attack the other for a distance of 2 miles above and 2 miles below. If 2 ships belonging to nations at war with each other are anchored there for trade and they both become ready to sail at the same time, they are not allowed to weigh anchor at the same time, but one of them must leave at least 24 hours before the other one. Therefore, ships for all the countries head for Fida, which is in effect a free harbour, and the slaves, which are the goods for which the greatest trade is carried on, cannot but be dearer and dearer.

It is true that Dapper writes somewhat about Popo, but he does not mention the kingdom of Fida, that has, indeed, for a long time been in a most favoured position, both because of its power as well as for the

---

45 *Benda*, the Akan name for a unit of gold dust, represents 2 ounces of gold dust.

intense slave trade that goes on there. It is 10 to 12 miles below, or east of, Popo, but above [west of] the kingdom of Harder [Allada].[46]

On this occasion I must write in greater detail about the merchants' trade //78// in that country, since it appears that trade in Guinea is now beginning to increase noticeably. Should you ask why this is so, one can readily cite many reasons, some of which are the number of forts and lodges, where the Negroes find far too much to choose from, so that if they do not want to pay the ordinary price for goods at one place, they can go to another a little further away. This is done, if not for personal gain, yet to harm others and win trade for themselves, [by taking it away] from others.

Much is very possibly by reason of the Dutch and English having far too close contact with the Blacks, who, by nature, are intelligent, and, particularly when it is to their own advantage, they are unbelievably sly, wily and cunning. They have become far too familiar and knowledgeable both about the worth of the goods, as well about weights and measures, so that they know almost as much as we do ourselves about the low prices of our European goods and the high value placed in Europe on their Guinean goods.

But the greatest damage to //79// trade, with out a doubt, is caused by the Dutch and English interlopers, who both can strike a better bargain than those at the forts can, and acquire whatever gold they can.[47] And these are the causes of the decrease in trade, but it is not easy to put a stop to it, since everyone works to his own advantage – according to the old proverb – following even older customs and acts in word and deed.

To prevent the Negroes from this kind of selfish activity is extremely difficult, indeed impossible since, because they cannot themselves come under the fortress with their goods – which is strictly forbidden to them – they entrust others in another *negeri* with their gold and goods, who, in turn, purchase [goods] for some 100 rixdaler, and then sell them somewhere else.

---

46  For a detailed description of the slave trade on the Slave Coast, see, in particular, Robin Law *The Slave Coast of Africa 1550-1750*, 1991, Ch. 5

47  Furthermore, interlopers did not have the expense of maintaining forts or lodges, so they could trade quickly in the roads, and move on. See L.F. Rømer *A Reliable Account of the Coast of Guinea* (1760) 40, n.34, 55, 189.

And because trade is with gold, you must be extremely on your guard in receiving the gold, both from Whites and Blacks. But especially the Negroes are highly expert in adulterating gold with silver, brass and copper, so that even those most experienced in [trading with] gold must truly depend on their hands, eyes, teeth and touchstones //**80**//, and even then you can hardly be sure that you will not be cheated.[48]

The Brazilian gold is much finer and darker in colour and appearance than the Guinean. But the Portuguese in Brazil are now beginning to be highly expert in adulterating it. I can write here of my own experience, since I have seen, in one delivery of gold, a piece of copper that was completely gilt weighed on a scale, and since I knew that a piece of gold of that size would always weigh more [than the scale showed], I tested it with a hammer to see if I could hammer it flat. This can always be done with gold, but it broke at the first stroke, and this showed it actually to be gilt copper, which the touchstone would scarcely have revealed.

Fraud is far more common here on the so-called Gold Coast, which actually cannot be considered to stretch farther than from Ankoper, a lodge under Axim, and down to Puni [?Kpone]. Admittedly, gold can be acquired – but very infrequently and in only small amounts – at Capo Verde, Rio Gambia, Capo Monte, Capo Mesurado, and //**81**// many other places below or to the east; but it is very poor and the inhabitants acquire it after many days' journey inland, and have themselves very little of it in the vicinity, so that [area] cannot be called Gold Coast. Likewise, at all the places and *negerier* which lie east of Aqvambus' lowest boundary, such as Aqvahu, Kræpe, Lampe, Qvita, Great and Small Popo, Fida and all the places to the east, or below, they have no gold, and much prefer, in trade and business, to receive payment in *bussies* rather than gold, with which they are not very familiar.[49]

One does, indeed, see gold among many people down there, but it is absolutely certain that all the gold found below Puni is either from a

---

48  A touchstone is a very smooth, fine-grained variety of quartz or jasper used to test the quality of gold or silver by the mark made when rubbed by the article being tested.

49  *Bussies/boss* refers to cowrie shells. The term is derived from the Portuguese *buzio*, a univalve snail shell.

particular trade transaction from Aqvambu – since the Aqvambus have acquired it first hand from Axim or Akani, where it is plentiful – or it is Brazilian gold, which the Portuguese or others, lacking bussies, gave as payment for their slaves and for whatever else they had to sell.[50]

//82// I have just written that gold is found in great quantities in Axim , or the Akanian gold mines. This must not lead one to assume that I, or any other European or Christian, could tell anything about this based on his own experience, or claim to have seen it himself, because no Christian man is even allowed to enter their territory. The Aqvambus, who are their neighbours, do go there to trade, but not without carrying guns, and only in limited numbers. They tell about incredibly large pieces of gold, weighing several stone or [up to] 36 pounds, that one or another of them can unexpectedly come upon in the mines. But such large pieces are not taken out. The largest piece of gold that I have ever seen in that size and appearance that has been found in the mines, weighed one pound. And it is extremely difficult to get such large lumps from the Negroes, so are purchased only rarely. This is not only because of the great value and high price for gold itself, but because they consider such large pieces to be their *fetis*. They consider it to be a god, and have great faith in it, therefore they would hardly part with it.

//83// It cannot be denied that the Akra Negroes, at times, after a great storm, can find a little gold in the sand on the beach. They usually work under the fortress, Christiansborg, with their flat pans, industriously rinsing the earth out in the lagoon in order to find the gold, which always sinks to the bottom. But it is just as certain that it is not worth the trouble, since they claim that they have acquired a great quantity when, after much work, they have only 12 *pfennig* worth after a whole day's work. And on many days they find nothing at all, so it is probable that Dapper must have been misinformed, according to what he reports.

I have been on the so-called rich 'Gold Mountain' in Commendo, described by Dapper, and there I have seen great holes and mines in the earth, remaining after the Negroes' work in past times. But it is

---

50  On the policy of the Akwamu hoarding gold, see Wilks *Akwamu 1640-1750*, 68-69.

unthinkable that the Dutch and the English, who have their forts at a half *fjerding mile's* distance from there would have left them untouched if they thought they could find it profitable to work and run the mines, unless they do it out of jealousy, and would rather lose both than allow the other to profit by it.[51]

//84// All the way along the coast of Guinea, from Capo Verde down to Akra, nothing other than gold is accepted as payment. This is very difficult for the poor Christians, since when an amount of gold worth one rigsdaler is to be divided into so many small amounts, and then is weighed in 9 or 10 parts, one can scarcely get 5 Danish marks for it. Those small pieces are called *kakras*, some worth 2, some 4 and some 8 pfennig, and it all depends on great care in the weighing if one is to avoid loss. But from, and including, Akra, and fairly far down the coast, *bussies* are the good [currency], and are sometimes preferred to gold.

After my promise given earlier, on page 38, I should now inform my readers, who might not have known it before, about what the oft-mentioned *bussies* are, since before I actually learned what *bussies* are I had seen them in many places in Denmark where they are called 'snake skulls'. There they are found as large as hens' eggs, used in many places in bell pulls beside people's beds and at their tables; I have certainly seen //85// them in other places, and even farmers in Denmark have them hanging on the straps of their money bags. Here in Guinea [I learned] that only the small white bussies are current, not the large brownish ones, with black marks and stripes, like the ones you find in Denmark. *Bussies* are small sea snail shells from the Maldives, and they are used at the above-named places as money and small coins. Of these *bussies* – which are called cowries – there are 10 to a shilling, 40 to a *damba*, and 80 to a *taku*, and so on.[52]

---

51 A *fjerding* = 1883 m.

52 The gold dust and cowrie systems were separate along the entire Guinea Coast apart from at Christiansborg, where the two systems met. Cf. Marion Johnson 'The cowrie currencies of West Africa', *Journal of African History* 11, 1970, 332.

# Chapter Eight

As for the inhabitants themselves, it must truly be reported about them that there are people on the coast of Guinea who have very bad habits and way of life. Yet they have a very high opinion of themselves, and walk with very proud gait and in a Spanish manner [sic]; but the best among them, indeed even their kings, act like beggars and paupers even though some of them are wealthy enough.

They are usually well-trained and expert in thievery and swindling, but they do not know how to read or write, and care nothing at all about it, because they say that their *fitis*, or idol, will not tolerate it; and so they continue, very lazy and indolent, absolutely content in such ignorance and coarseness.

//86// Regarding their knowledge of God, or the Highest Being, it is sadly lacking, and they treat the subject with a remarkable nonchalance. If one asks them about their *fitis*, or God, whom they believe in and in whom they place their trust, they do not know themselves what name to give him at all times. Sometimes it is one thing, at other times another; at times they make it a piece of gold, at others a tiger paw, then a parrot feather, suddenly an iron chain, or whatever their imagination comes up with at the moment to be their idol. They are, in this matter, so absolutely inconsistent that they create, daily or weekly, some other god. The Akras call god *Jungo*, and the Aqvambues call god *Jankumpung*.[53] They admit, and know, that Satan exists, whom they credit as being very powerful, but Satan is considered to be an ill-humoured and stubborn man, and [they believe] that it is necessary to have the devil as a friend. Yet, they admit that God is capable of much

---

53  In Ga, *Nyoŋmo* ; in Akan *O-nyankopoŋ*.

more than Satan in the government and outcome of all things, be they good or bad. They believe that both God and the devil are people whom we Christians know, but they do not themselves; //87// indeed they are of the opinion that they have no great need to know Him [sic], therefore they do not worry much about it.

Concerning the movement of the heavens and the changes of time dependent upon that [movement] they have no understanding, nor do they wish to know anything about it, or about anything that does not affect them.[54] Yet, in their own manner, they do know about the *Bon Dies* and *Mal Dies*, which names they utter according to their own way of speaking in broken Portuguese. From this we can surmise that they have received their superstition and poor understanding not from their own people's forefathers, but purely from the Portuguese, from the time when they [the Portuguese] first began to sail to the country. They reckon when their *Bon Dies*, or lucky days come, as [the days] when they can undertake important transactions, such as waging war, planting millie, and such things. However, when their *Mal Dies*, their unlucky or inauspicious days come, they are never able to undertake anything of importance.[55]

They care absolutely nothing about thunder and lightning, indeed almost less than dumb animals do, who at times are very frightened by this. But, since storms happen so frequently among these heathens, it is as if they //88// have not heard it. When asked what they think about them, or how they judge them, they answer, with laughter, that God is *bringaring*, or celebrating, and enjoying himself with his *kabuseers*, or his prominent men; [56] and just as they hear that we Europeans fire guns from the ships or forts, they think thunder is the same thing, and say that God is a grand gentleman, or a Big Man, who has many guns and much powder, which is what we are told. They call the Christians' priests *sopho*, meaning, in their wickedness, that these

---

54 The fact they they are living near the equator where the days and nights are of equal length all year round undoubtedly plays a role in this 'nonchalance'.

55 Rask has no knowledge of the calendar systems on the Coast . The Ga calendar is based on the lunar month; the Akan on a cycle of 42 days. Many calendar systems have their auspicious and inauspicious days.

56 *Kabuseer/kabossie* is from the Portuguese *caboceiro*, 'head man'.

are the Christians' daily gods here on earth, just as their own various, and almost daily changing, [gods] are.[57]

The Christians, especially those who keep them in awe, and consequently do some good things for them, are held in great respect and honour; and for those whom they wish to show special honour, they throw themselves flat onto the ground and wipe the shoe soles [of the one being honoured] with the hair of their own head. And this is done not only by slaves or others of low rank of the poor among them, but even by the greatest *kabuseers*, who are to them like the nobility are to us.

//89// They show the greatest humility to their kings in outward signs of respect. When they come before their king they throw themselves down and crawl on the ground towards him, and now and then they clap their hands; then they state their errand or request while lying on the ground in front of him.

---

57  ɔsɔfo is the Akan term for a priest.

# Chapter Nine

Their king is no more than a member of the leading *kabuseers'* family. In some places, since there are many such, they might own 3-400 inherited slaves whom they can lead out into the war as their soldiers, or their army, besides a number of unfree [*sic*] slaves to carry their loads as necessary, [working] at their houses, or camps when they are at war. Established camps are never used. They do not know how [to set them up] but only raise some reed and straw huts, which they set on fire when they break camp.

They never practise military order, nor do any form of fighting against each other in an upright position, but usually attack, sometimes with 100, sometimes with 1,000 men. Then, when they arrive at the arena, or battlefield, they crawl through grass and undergrowth with remarkable //**90**// speed, until they see that they can successfully take a life. The *kabuseer* who, with his soldiers, performs well, and brings down the greatest number of his enemy, is called *Abringpung*, that is, a prominent gentleman and hero; or *Aurangfrang*, that is, one who is accomplished in using a gun. But the one who has lost is called *Obia*, that is, a woman.[58]

When they plan to wage war on each other, their kings summon their [own] *kabuseers*, to meet, each with his own men, who number 200, sometimes 300, sometimes 400, and even more men in the field, with their own military equipment and provisions. However, each *kabuseer* has his own special banner, and every group has its own field insignia, so that they can identify one another. If they force their enemy to flee, they follow him with horrible screams.

---

58  The terms are Akan: *abringpung/obrempong*, chief; *obia/obéa*, woman.

They have remarkable military attire. They are all naked, apart from a strip of cloth about 3 *alen* long and 2 *alen* wide, which they fold like a neck scarf, then wrap it around their waist, with one part between their thighs, so that one end is in the middle //**91**// in back, and the other end in the middle in front. On top of this they wear a belt of white leather about 4 fingers wide. Between this and their naked bodies they stick their swords, placed so that they are fastened almost up under their arms. On the left side of the belt is their cartridge box, which is very neatly formed with 18-20 cartridges inside. On the belt they also hang a pouch containing their bullets, of which few are cast in lead; and since they have no bullet moulds it is reported that they have no particular use for lead bullets in war or when they go hunting for elephants or other large animals. Instead, they hammer out long, round, iron rods, as thick as a curtain rod, or as the outermost joint of the little finger. These are then cut into many pieces, about the size of a bullet – not round but oblong – by which they think they have a sharper shot, which they do, in truth, because when they hit something with such a bullet, it tears a large piece of flesh, making a dangerous wound. However they can hardly send off a precise shot with such bullets //**92**// at long range. Furthermore, they usually do not all aim as we do, but only let it go as soon as they feel they have the target right close to them. And with that kind of iron bullets they ruin and explode many a good musket. On their heads, on such campaigns, they wear a straw cap, very pretty, and finely woven, [?worth] 1 or 2 *taku* – that is 8 shillings or 1 Danish mark – decorated with one or several long feathers in the top, which is their most valued ornamentation. Others make caps for themselves out of the hides of small animals, others throw a monkey hide, from which the small legs have been cut off, loosely over their heads, believing that they are, thus, well protected.

Their kings cannot wage war without the agreement and support of their *kabuseers*. Indeed, it happens often that a *kabuseer* can wage war on the king on a very flimsy excuse. The kings in that country have absolutely no certain income from their subjects, but live off the millie plants and the palm trees; that is to say that they have bread and a drink of palm wine or only water. However, should [a king] have a case against any of them, //**93**// he punishes them severely in their pocketbooks. Yet, since the King of Aqvambu has seen the examples both of the Akras' as well as the Qvahus' kings – which showed that by their harsh treatment and behaviour toward their *kabuseers* and other subjects, they found themselves so helpless and hated by their people, that they had to pay with both land and life – he has learnt to fare more mildly with his subjects, mostly with the Aqvambus, since the Akras and the Qvahus, who are both his vassals now, have been totally suppressed, and deprived of all their might, so that he has not much to fear from them in any way.[59]

---

59  For the history of the Akwamu emergence as a coastal power, see Ivor Wilks *Akwamu 1640-1750,* 7-14.

# Chapter Ten

That, then, was a short description of their method of waging war; of how they arm themselves; what their daily food and provisions consist of; in short, millie is their bread, just as grain is normally ours. And it is a fact that they can prepare very good, tasty bread of millie.But besides that, from millie they can brew good beer, called *ahaj*.[60] At Qvita, Popo, Harder and Fida they brew such beer, and store it in large clay pots in the earth //**94**// to preserve it, well covered with earth. After a period of 2 or 3 months, it can be so strong and so tasty that it can easily make a fellow right intoxicated when he drinks it. However, there must be so many gathered in the company that that large clay pot of *ahaj* can be emptied then and there, since what is left over becomes rotten once the pot has been opened. It becomes sour immediately, so that on the next day no one can drink it. Besides the millie beer, or *ahaj*, palm wine is the preferred and best that they usually drink. It can, at times, be very good, and is not unhealthy for those who are used to it. Indeed, I have found out myself that palm wine is an excellent treatment for those who are plagued by stone.

As regards foodstuffs Akra is very poor, almost infertile, and consequently a very expensive place, where a chicken normally costs 24 to 28 shillings, a pig 12 to 14 rigsdaler, and I have seen a *gjeld-væder* [ram], as they are called in Denmark, which was only moderately large, but nicely fat, for which they //**95**// took 3 *pesos* or 12 rigsdaler; a cow costs 1 *benda* or 32 rigsdaler – unless you haggle. A Danish *pot* measure of *ahaj* – which is not especially good here in comparison to that in

---

60  *Ahai* is basically a non-alcoholic beverage made from maize (M:E: Kropp Dakubu *Ga-English Dictionary*1999). Clearly, it has been fermented here.

the places mentioned above – costs 1 *damba,* or 4 shillings. While I have been here, one might be willing to pay 1 ounce [of gold dust] or 16 rigsdaler for one and one-half *lispund* of Dutch or English butter, and still not be able to buy it.[61] Cows and sheep are not milked here, so that there is absolutely no butter in this land, but you must make do, instead, with palm oil for your food, if you cannot purchase butter from the ships. An *anker* of French brandy usually costs 16 rigsdaler, an *ahme* of ordinary French wine fetches 8 to 10 pesos, and, at times, a good 3 ounces or 48 rigsdaler;[62] an oxhead of red wine, if it is good, costs, according to the going price, 2 *benda,* 2 *pesos,* or 72 rigsdaler, a bottle of English ale of 3½ *pegel* costs 4 *taku* or 2 Danish marks, and even, at times, 6 *taku,* or 3 marks.[63] All this I have noted down in some detail, //**96**// from which you can better understand that it is very expensive to live here.

At this point I must report what has been told to me, with great assurance, that among the Qvahus there are truly found so-called anthropophagi, or those who slaughter people as food. I write this as it was told to me, and for my part I dare not doubt the descriptions that were given to me, but require no one to accept this.

At other places, such as Aqvambu, Akani, Asiante, Agona, Qvahu, at Qvita, Popo, and below [further east] that stretch inland, there are very fertile areas, with a greater abundance of foodstuffs. But since I shall continue to write about the products of this land, I cannot refrain from noting, as I have seen it, and since I am somewhat acquainted with the true iron ore in Norway, I am certain that the earth at all the high places in Akra appears to show that the finest iron one could wish for could be worked in abundance if there could be found the necessary supplies of water //**97**// with which to work it – all other things being equal.

Next I shall touch on some information about the fruits of the land, [fruits] found at the fertile places. I shall not here write of *pisang* and *bakoves,* which have been described before, but of *lailap,*

---

61  *Lispund* = 16 pounds.

62  *Ahme/ame* is an old liquid measure, signifying c. 4 ankers, or casks.

63  *Taku,* an Akan weight = 80 cowries.

without a doubt the same fruit that Dapper calls *foles,* according to the description he gives. The Negroes call them *lailap,* and the Dutch *Cormantin apples,* because they resemble very small apples, and are supposed, as I am told, to grow in great quantities particularly at the Dutch fortress Cormantin.

*Jammes* [yams] are a variety of root, which produces only a little green above ground. Of these roots, however, there can be found some that weigh 14 to 16 pounds, and they are not unhealthy to eat, so that we eat them often instead of bread. The English give their slaves *jammes* every other day, instead of millie or bread.

*Akros* is a variety of root that is somewhat larger than the largest grey peas.[64] They send a very few leaves above ground, but the roots spread very wide and lie like small nuts that have been set out //98// on a thread a little way one from the other. We find these roots especially useful since they can be stored for a good half year, and when you take half a handful of them, crush them in water as you do with millie – which shall be described later – then put the crushed dough into a deep bowl with enough water that it resembles a porridge, stir it a few times, wring the liquid out of it through a cloth, and bring it to a boil, then, when it is cold, it tastes very much like a thick sheep's milk. We use this *akros* milk often as a fine dish, it is nourishing, but causes wind.

*Papai* [pawpaw] is a fairly good fruit. At times it is found as large as an ordinary coconut. It has a thin, smooth skin, just like large cucumbers at their smoothest. When it is fully ripe it begins to turn somewhat yellow. Inside the green skin is the meat, about an inch thick, and dark, flame-gold in colour. Inside of this there are 2 spoonfuls of small black eyes, floating in an either poor-tasting or tasteless slime, which must be cleaned out because it is of no use. Then you take //99// the juice of *brambas,* that is small Guinean limes, and mix the meat of the *papai* with it, so you can eat it. But it tastes neither sweet and lovely, nor is it healthy. If you drink water too soon after [eating it], which is the most common drink, you will soon experience heartburn. The *papai*

---

64  The description resembles that of tiger nuts, but the name in Ga or Twi is nothing like *akros* (p.c. M.E. Dakubu).

tree grows very quickly, but does not exceed a height of more than 12 to 16 feet. It stands for only a few years before it dies. It is very loose and full of sap, the wood is very bitter, and [the tree] resembles the crown of the herb dill. The branches and leaves, which are very wide, sit outermost on the ends of the branches, but the fruit, which can be 20 to 30 in number on a fully grown tree, sit on the stem, close up to the crown, very close to each other, yet each on its own stem.

The palm tree, of whose oil I shall write about mainly – and which I know very well – that same oil is extracted both from the small as well as the large palm nuts. The small ones are very red, as large as good-sized rose hips or *nyper*, as we //**100**// call them in Norway. These small nuts sit in between the lowest layer of branches of the tree, totally hidden, so that they cannot be seen before some of those branches are cut off. There is a hard stone in each of the small red nuts. 12 to 16 of these small nuts, when they have been cooked, taste oily and good, and because of their fat [content] they cause a gentle evacuation. Palm oil is also extracted from the large nuts that grow on the branches of the palm tree, and are as large as a perfect goose egg. This oil is used in many ways, both for eating and in their healing practices, which have, to a degree, been described before. Then there is palm wine, which is considered to be among the most excellent of drinks.[65] This is acquired in abundance, thus is obtainable for a tolerable price, but it does not taste good to those who are not accustomed to it; nor is it found everywhere. As a remedy against a tendency to stone, it is absolutely marvellous. Anyone can thus note very easily, from all this, how wonderfully useful the palm tree is in a great number of ways.

Sugar cane usually grows in great quantities //**101**// where there is damp earth. It grows, at times, to a height and length of 3 to 4 *alen*, and can be found to be as thick as a man's wrist. It grows tall very quickly, and is divided into many joints on the stem, about a quarter *alen* apart from each other. The shell, or bark, is green and smooth, tough and somewhat hard. The sugar juice is in the cane, in a spongy marrow, and that kind of cane inside the shell, is far looser and juicier than a cabbage stalk after it has been peeled.

---

65  For tapping methods see Isert (1788/1992) 168-9; *idem* (2007) 223-4.

Cotton bushes also grow there in great numbers. In appearance they are like the wild bushes in Denmark, since they spread out into numerous branches in the same way, but are scarcely higher than a man. The cotton sits outermost on the branches in round pods like a peony. When the pod is fully ripe, it bursts open of itself, and there is the wool, which is very white, as large as good-sized fist, or a large powder puff.

In the areas described above they harvest twice a year, provided there is normal rainfall. However, at Akra they suffer, at times, //**102**// from a great lack [of rain], particularly during the hot season that usually lasts from the beginning of the month of June to the month of March.

# Chapter Eleven

And now I shall record what kind of animals are found in this country. There are cattle, but normally they are only very small, nor are they found in very great numbers; which could indeed be increased if only the people in this country bothered to breed them. They do not milk their cattle, which seems strange to us, but there is a natural cause: the milk would taste absolutely disgusting, due to the strong-smelling plants that grow everywhere in the fields. That even makes the meat of the slaughtered animals taste so foul that one can hardly eat it, as has been mentioned earlier.

There are also sheep that, in like manner, are not milked. They usually lamb, or produce lambs, twice a year, or about 2 every 15 months.

Regarding goats in this country, there are 2 kinds. One variety is very like a deer in physical appearance, and is almost as long-legged. This variety rarely gives birth to more than 2 kids at a time. The other variety, however, is short-legged, and often gives birth to 4 kids at a //103// time, although it can scarcely feed and raise 3 of them. But, just as it is the case with cattle and sheep, the same must be said about goats, that they do not milk them here.

There are also horses on the coast of Guinea, but they are very small. Furthermore, they are very poor, in total contrast to our Norwegian horses, which are usually very lively, plucky and good-natured, while theirs lack both good physical form and spirit. Nor do they make any attempt to raise their horses. I never saw any even moderately handsome horses there. But whether this is due to lack of knowledge among the people, or negligence due to not knowing how to treat a horse, or [whether it is due to] the heat and the kind of fodder, I cannot say with any certainty.

On the other hand there are many elephants. But, since my position did not allow me to travel or journey farther inland from the fortress and the seashore, I was never able to see a living elephant. [But I did see] one that was dried. Behind Crevecoeur's *negeri*, called Akra, there lies a dried, unbelievably large, skull and jaw bones of an elephant, from which one can conclude their enormous size.

//**104**// Our drum major, Christian Whit tells of an incident that he himself experienced once when he was out hunting a couple of miles inland from Christiansborg. He became aware of a herd of elephants, but since they ferociously chase after people in the fields , he did not dare attempt to shoot any of them unless he could get around them; so he decided to climb up into a tree and keep watch, to wait for an opportunity to do so. But then, when he was trying to run around them as fast as he could, he fell into a hole in the thick grass that was actually the footprint of an elephant. He came across holes like this throughout the entire valley, since wherever an elephant steps in the soft and swampy earth, it leaves a footprint that is like a small well. It was into such a hole that Christian Whit sank right up to his armpits in mud and water, and had to go home, muddy and wet, his purpose unfulfilled. He assured me, too – which was also confirmed by our chief merchant Mr. Knud Rost, who had once, down near Qvita, //**105**// seen a herd of 12 elephants – that, when coming so aggressively. a male is always in the lead; and as soon as he is aware of people he gives forth a very audible sign. He blows through his trunk so that it sounds louder than a trumpet, and thus sounds a warning.

The elephants have very wide and very flat ears that hang down, which the Negroes sell for a low price. As a test I once bought an elephant ear from a Negro. It was as dry and hard as the best English embossing leather, and I had made a perfect pair of shoe soles that were so extraordinarly strong that they could not be worn out.

Their tails are very short in comparison to their very large bodies. The important *kabuseers* usually use them for special ornamentation since the largest hair [of the tail] is so thick and large, but somewhat longer, than that of the largest wing feather of a raven when that has been plucked. And that is what it resembles most closely. The Negresses willingly pay 6 or 8 shillings for one of the hairs, or brushes, because they fasten them in the curled hair lock as a large decoration, according to their own fashion.//**106**// I shall not write any more about the many things I have been told as true about the elephant, since those things have been described by others.

The *ur-bull*, or wild beast [buffalo?] is found in great numbers and size up in the country, and are so very ferocious that the *ur-bull* is considered by the Negroes to be far more aggressive and dangerous to meet than an elephant, since the elephant can very eagerly pursue a hunter who has shot at him, but if the person climbs up into a tree, the elephant goes his way immediately, thinking that it was honourable enough and sufficient revenge that he has driven his intended attacker to flight. But the *ur-bull* is faster in his pursuit of a person, even one who has not injured him, and furthermore, as soon as the person is able to escape by climbing a tree, he attacks the tree violently, trying to shake [the person] down. He scrapes the earth, and strives to show his great rage, and if this does not work, the *ur-bull* will stay in the grass around the tree for 3 days and nights, so that the person can not preserve his life in any way, //**107**// unless, either thirst forces the animal to go away, or the person can watch to see when the ox lies down and he can be certain that it is asleep. Which gives me the opportunity to believe that God's spirit is like our Lord Christ's enemies, and pursuers by oxen and wild oxen of Basan: psalm 22.13.[66] *Great oxen have surrounded me, fat oxen have lain around me.* If others have come upon this same thought is unbeknown to me.

Wild pigs are also found there in great numbers, and are both large and dangerous. I have been told much about them by the Blacks, but I have noted that it has all been told by others, so I shall not occupy myself by describing them.

Porcupines are not lacking, either, on the Guinea Coast. There are 2 kinds. One that is a larger variety – but many who have already written

---

66  This is 22.12 in the King James version: '*Many bulls have encompassed me: strong bulls of Bashan have beset me round.*'

about them have described them as somewhat larger than those actually found. I have seen a dead one of that variety, whose longest spines were not more than 10 inches long. The Negroes have told me that the sore caused by that spine – with which [the animal] defends itself against anyone who tries to attack it //**108**// by shooting all of them out of its hide – is very difficult to heal, but not impossible. The Blacks shoot them when they find them, and eat them with great pleasure, as the most delicious game. They are difficult to find since they have their homes and hiding places deep underground. The small porcupines are found in the fields, and they closely resemble those that are found in Denmark. And just as the small ones do, the large porcupines roll themselves [into a ball].

There are harts and hinds just as in Denmark, but they have 2 kinds, both large, that are like those we know in Europe.[67] But there is a variety of hart and hind that is very small; whose legs, when they are fully grown, are no larger or thicker, with hide and hair, than the legs of a small, one-month-old kid. And the legs of this kind of deer are usually plated with gold on the end, and used as tobacco tampers.

Hares are found here in great numbers, but they are smaller than the Norwegian hares, although those in Norway are clearly smaller than those in Denmark. But the hares, as well //**109**// as other kinds of game in Guinea, are found rarely, both because the animals are really difficult to shoot, and because the Negroes are lazy and poor hunters as regard shooting [?this kind of] game.

The animal *qvuoggelo* is called *oderong* by the Akras. I have had a young one that was 4 feet long [?as a pet]. It is not at all poisonous, having as its food and nourishment nothing but ants. Sometimes it is found up in the tallest trees, running onto the outermost branches. It has no fear of falling both because it has been equipped by nature with very long and sharp claws, and because it always gets a grip around the branches with its long and flat tail, by which it can hold itself fast. When it wants to move from one branch to another it hangs firmly by its tail until it can reach the branch it is aiming for with its paws, and can grasp it. It can roll itself up as if bound by a rope, and can protect its

---

67 Hart and hind are the male and female of the red deer.

head and feet in that roll so that nothing can harm them. It has no hide or hair, as do other four-footed animals, nor does it have spines like a porcupine, but from the head to //**110**// the tail – and except for the head and tail – it has a thick shell and scales, far harder and thicker than that of a lobster; yet, just as on the body of the lobster, the scales go in under one another, almost in the same way as in an iron coat of armour, so that the second shell goes under the first and the third under the second when it turns and moves. It is almost unbelievable to what length it can stretch itself, since, when it walks it looks short; but when it rolls itself up [*sic*], or hangs in the trees by its tail, as described above, it stretches itself so much longer, so that one would not believe it is the same animal.[68]

There are found a multitude of varieties of monkeys all over the Coast, but even many more farther inland, and it appears that the Almighty and one and only wise Creator, who has determined the living space of every kind of creature and animal, wished, with these immodest, unclean, ugly and destructive animals, to put to shame the degenerate inhabitants of this land. During the time I lived in that land I was shown many kinds of monkeys, //**111**// but I have not seen any kind that I deemed should, or could be, tolerated, much less loved, since they are all very unclean, and cause damage to everything they find. Moreover they are so immoral, and especially the males are so shameless, that no honourable person can see them without blushing for shame.

The Negroes assure me that when they travel inland and their path is near or around rivers where these beasts mostly stay because of the water, they must just as much, and even more, fear a flock of monkeys and baboons. The latter are very unlike the others, as regards both size, fur and physical appearance, yet they are all of the same species and get on well together, as a flock of tigers do, regardless of their cruelty and greed. The monkeys are both unbelievably swift to attack, and are usually far more numerous, as well as having a very bad bite; and for those that are the very worst, their bite is very difficult to heal. It is difficult to drive them away, since more and more of them come out

---

68 Probably the pangolin.

of their hollows and //112// distant caves as soon as some of them scream. But, when they have to take flight, it is most entertaining to see how those who have young who cannot run so fast, and wishing to follow their mothers they hang, 2 or 3 of them – they usually do not have more at each [birth] – on the back or under the belly of the mother, and she must thus drag them along and preserve them from danger.

# Chapter Twelve

There are many varieties of birds there, displaying the Mighty Creator's and Sustainer's boundless wisdom and inscrutable providence. There are especially many turtle doves who, in every way, are like ours in Europe.

Pheasants are found there in great numbers, remarkably larger than those we have in our country. This has been mentioned before, and it is because this part of the world is their natural fatherland, while in our country they are strangers, and do not reach their natural size.

Parrots of notably varying feathers, colours, types and sizes are found in great numbers. But on the Guinea Coast they are mostly blue-grey, and many of them are brought to us from inland. But //113// although one must admit that they are especially clever and learn to talk and whistle very quickly, and they are also stronger than the other sort in being able to travel far over the sea, there is little or nothing about them that is pleasing to see, apart from the lovely red feathers in their tails. The Negroes eagerly purchase these feathers, especially when [the birds] are only half-grown, paying at times 2, or even 4 shillings apiece, and they use them to set into their fetishes, around their necks or on their heads.

Otherwise, the Negroes, especially when they come down from the Akanist country, bring, in small baskets, a variety of small parrot, which the Dutch call *parachities* [parakeets]. They are green in colour, and have bodies no larger than a lark. At times a pair can be purchased for one *taku*, or 8 shillings, but they are of no use other than to be looked at. They do not tolerate cold at all, for which reason I hardly think they can be seen at all north of Italy, much less in our northernmost kingdoms. We had more than 50 of them on the English warship, //114// *Falmuth*, with which I travelled to Europe, but as soon as we came a bit north and could just begin to feel the cold, they all died, one after the other.

Of the grey parrots there are also a great many: one can, at times, see 1,000 of them down at Capo de Lopo Gonsalvas, from which they fly in great flocks over the sea to Isle de Prince [Principe] , Isle de St. Thoma [São Thomé]. I understand the [latter] to be the large island St. Thomas, which lies under the æquinoctial line, and is reckoned to be 20 miles long and nearly as wide. It belongs to the Portuguese, and is an excellent land, with markets, churches, cloisters, and it enjoys considerable income. These same grey parrots fly over to Anna Bona, indeed, even farther; at times one sees them even at Isle de Ferdinando [Fernando Po].

The Brazilian parrots are usually green, and are considered to be the most rare, but the farther north one comes in America, the larger and more blue they become, and are good for nothing other than to be eaten //115// – and they are not unpleasant to eat. In the road at Barbados I saw one on an English warship that had come from Salem in New England, a parrot as large in body as a well-grown young hen.

There are *skader*, but in Guinea they are somewhat smaller than ours, and they are brown on their backs and black under the belly.[69] Nor are they seen to go after carrion, as do ours, and it seems to me that it must be a larger variety of the bird called shrike in Denmark, because they resemble it most in the beak, which is somewhat curved, but the tail is somewhat too long.

There are plenty of sparrows and other small birds, but they are of no value because they are almost mute, as regards song. I can never remember hearing a beautiful bird song on the entire coast of Guinea. In contrast, one cannot walk in the forest in our country, in spring and summer, without hearing the woods filled with many kinds of small wild birds singing lively songs.

Otherwise, in Akra, there is a small bird, //116// somewhat smaller

---

69  *Skade* (*Pica caudata*) is a bird of the raven family, having a hoarse cry, a very long, pointed tail, and is very active.

than a sparrow, that changes colour and feathers 3 times a year. At one time it is brown on its back and black-grey under the belly, at another time it is completely raven-black, and at a third time it is bright red on the back and around the neck, but blackish under the belly. It is found in very great numbers, with this difference, that some of them, which are undoubtedly males, have 2 feathers in their tail, rounded and a quarter [?alen] long, which they strike together when they are flying, thus giving forth a strange sound that hums in the air. The Negroes are convinced that if you eat the meat of this bird you can get sleeping sickness from it. Clearly this is pure imagination, and is not true at all: because after I first gave my Boy some of the meat to eat, and noted that he took no injury of it, both the governor, Mr. Frans Boje, and I ate it several times thereafter, without experiencing the least discomfort.

Since I have mentioned sleeping sickness, I cannot avoid telling how common it is in these countries, //117// and that it kills many of the Blacks.[70] But we have not yet heard of any Christians at these places having suffered from it. It is more common and more injurious for the slaves, who, when they have become infected, fall asleep immediately, while sitting or even standing still; and when they have had this illness for a couple of years, they lose their desire to eat, whereupon they waste away daily, and yet sleep regularly, until they sleep their lives away. I have noticed with two of them who have become affected with this weakness, that during the last 8 or 14 days, when one could see that this would be a certain death, they were well as long as they were left to sleep quietly. But as soon as you tried to waken them and make them get up, it was as if a disturbance in their senses caused a terrible shivering and a trembling motion, like a form of that 'falling sickness' [epilepsy], as it is called in Norway, except that they do not clench their fists. [They have] as little advice or cure for this illness as they know the cause or reason for it. It is strange that no one else is affected //118// by this illness than slaves and servants.

The bird which is the size of a turtle dove, that Dapper calls tonga, the name the Blacks on the Gold Coast give it, is not known to me.

---

70  Any of several similar illnesses caused by protozoans of the genus Trypanosoma, Transmitted by flies.

Our Deputy Assistent, Niels Hansøn, who told me about it, has seen it in great numbers hanging from the branches of the palm trees and coconut trees in the Fida country. They are not seen in the daytime because they do not fly out until the evening, so that every evening, in clear and dry weather, these birds are seen close under Christiansborg's walls.[71] They have very short legs, which I noticed on one that Peter von Wovern, one of our soldiers, had shot out in the fields where it was hanging under the branches of a tree. It is strange that when it sets down on the ground it is never in grass. Perhaps because of their short legs they would not be able to take flight. But one always sees them in the evening on bare patches of ground, where there is no grass; or they set down on a stone, and //**119**// when they make a flight either over the *negeri* or around the fortress, they always land in the same place. They are not particularly afraid of people because they are not sought by anyone, since they are of no use at all, and have in common with all other species of nocturnal birds that all such creatures are not worth shooting or capturing.

The small, yellowish bird that Dapper says resembles the Dutch gold finch is found in great numbers in Akra, and I can truly say that it is the only kind of bird that I have heard chirp and sing. In the places where they wish to build, and find it peaceful, there could be found 30 to 40 pairs in a tree, if it is large enough for that. In the innermost court at Christiansborg fortress there is a tree of average size – brought in from the fields and planted there in late Chief Merchant Mejer's time – in which, every year, in the months of June, July and August, more than 30 nests are built.[72] And one must acknowledge the great wisdom of the Creator that nature has taught these birds a very clever way of building. They fasten their nests under the branches of a coconut, or other leafy tree, and [by using] the softest grass straw //**120**// they know how to work and knot them together artistically so that they hang and swing in the wind, like the very largest pears in size, pointed at the top and round at the bottom. They have only one opening by which to enter the nest, and that is in the middle of the side, so that

---

71  Probably the night jar (Serle and Morel, 118 ff.).

72  For descriptions of weaver birds, see Serle and Morel 241-261.

their eggs and young lie in the round hollow in the bottom of the nest, as if in a powder bag – which the nest most resembles – where they are very safe and well-protected against rain and storm and whatever else might want to hurt them. These birds stay as fearlessly among people as do swallows in our country. The male is mostly yellow, except for some black on the head, but the female is brown on the back and pale grey under the belly. On the island Anna Bona I saw some of the same type of bird.

In the city of St. Michael, on Barbados, there was also a type of bird, in great numbers, that built in the same way, but they were black and as large as a starling, of which [species] I believe they are a member, since they resemble them so closely as regards movement and size.

At Akra there are only few large birds because of the lack of forest where they could //**121**// live and hide. But there are eagles, and of the kind that are the true eagle, in Guinea, they are larger than those found in our country; and in the places [on their bodies] where they are blackish brown in our country, the Guinean variety are more grey.

Another variety of eagle is found there that is smaller than ours, and is called *Malabar Birds*. The Dutch call them *stront-vogels* because of their extreme uncleanliness which, in the hot countries, causes a stench that follows them wherever they stay. They are very heavy and sluggish in flight, and no larger than a fully grown turkey hen, with pale yellow feet. The head is completely bare and bluish, like the head one would see on a dead turkey. These *Malabar Birds* are seen here in fairly great numbers.[73]

Kites are found there, and are, in every way, size and feathers like those we have in Denmark. Kites are especially numerous in Akra during the entire year, except during the *sinkesu-time*, when there comes a variety of fish (that I have described earlier, on pp. 7 and 19) in June and July, and sometimes in August, at which time kites are not seen on the coast, but they move //**122**// inland, to the forest, in order to breed. Thus, the Negroes have their unmistakeable sign that as soon as they notice that the kites have become fewer at the coast, they are certain that the fish *sinkesu* is coming, and they prepare to go

---

73  Probably a vulture.

fishing. On the contrary, when that bird returns and is again found on the coast, they need no other proof that the above-mentioned *sinkesu* presence is coming to an end.

Crows are not lacking there, either. However, even though they are very much like ours in size and sound, yet they are quite different in colour, since they are black and white where our crows are black and grey.

Storks are found there, too, and especially at the Rio Volta – which is several miles below Christiansborg – they are found in great numbers. However, they are the fetish of the Negroes who live there, and are considered to be a holy object which no one is permitted to touch or do it harm.[74] The same is the case with snakes at Fida – where the snakes are a fathom long and more – and they move quite tamely among the people in the daytime, and lie in their beds at night; //**123**// and one notes with wonder that they do not bite or harm the people. But even if they did, one must not harm the snake, which is considered to be sacred.[75]

In the Rio Volta there are caimans in great numbers, which are creatures that resemble pictures of crocodiles. It is a large, greedy and very harmful animal, which can live both on land and in water. It is commonly claimed to be the tiger's enemy. The hide is extremely hard and strong, used by the Blacks to cover their shields, when they can overpower a caiman and kill it.

Everywhere there are very great numbers of tiger-animals and bush dogs: the latter are undoubtedly a variety of over-grown wolves.[76] They often do great damage both to people and cattle. Just as Dapper reports that travellers in the kingdom of Senegal, every night, when they are going to make camp, must build a fire in order to frighten and drive away wild and ferocious animals, so do they do the same at Akra and everywhere else, I have been told, because of tigers and bush dogs. Without fire //**124**// and torches, well-loaded guns and strong company, they dare not travel.

---

74  This may be the Crowned Crane, *Balearica pavonina* (Serle and Morel 63, pl.11).

75  The snake referred to here is the python. For worship, see Isert (1788/1992) 106-107/144-45.

76  Very likely jackals.

The tree called *barrouv* is plentiful in Akra and everywhere. It has been described by Dapper, so I shall not repeat that here, but I have never seen nor heard of either people or cattle making use of the sap or the wood, because there are many other varieties of soft trees found in that country, which are of no use as firewood; but the turtle doves, of which there are also very great numbers, usually live in such trees. We call them *milk trees* because of the white and oily juice that is found throughout the leaves, bark and wood itself.

# Chapter Thirteen

At Akra very good salt is produced by the sun, which ranks no lower than European salt – even the best variety – in respect of its excellence; and the fierce heat of the sun and the high price forbids extravagant use of it [sic], but not because of a lack of salt. It is readily available, since both at the lagoon under Crevereour's *negeri*, as well as a stone's throw from Christiansborg, and mostly at Labade – which lies barely a half mile below Christiansborg – in the warmest period, //**125**// in the months of December, January and February, the Negroes produce it in great quantities. The so-called lagoons do not have their sources from inland streams and rivers, nor is their flow to the sea constant or regular; but, when they are quite full of fresh water, which usually happens at the end of the rainy season – when in some places the sandbanks break up where they are loosest and most sandy – the seawater pours in in strong currents, until the sea has washed in so much sand that the mouth of the lagoon is again closed. This usually happens late in the month of June. That salty water remains stagnant during the dry season, from June to December, and during that time, the drier it is, the greater the quantity and the better the salt that is obtained in the following way. From the flat and hard ground at the lagoon the Negroes take up small pieces of that surface, 8 to 10 feet long and 4 to 5 feet wide. They smear and enclose these pieces with good clay, to a thickness of, at the most, 4 inches. Then, using calabash containers, they remove the water that has been stagnant in the lagoon so long, and pour it into the //**126**// encased pieces on the sand; where because of the sun-heated water, in a space of 3 days, it becomes salt. This is then scraped off and put into reed sacks that they dip up and down in the lagoon until sand and all the impurities have been rinsed off, and then it is lovely, clear, hard salt. Immediately they fill the salt flats with water again, as before, and continue thus throughout the above-mentioned months.

We see the Aqvambuish Negroes come down daily, in numbers of 40 to 50, to buy such salt, as well as dried fish from the Akras. They carry it the long way back, frequently a journey lasting 8 to 10 days, to at least 50 miles inland, where it is sold for slaves and *pankis* for great profit.[77]

It is a fact that that well-known trader, Nicolaj Hansøn – who lived at Christianshavn, and in his time managed all the Danish trade, both at Tranqvebar in East India, St. Thoma in West India, Great Fridericsberg and Christiansborg in Guinea, but who finally met his end and lost both his life and his ship between //**127**// Skudesnæs and Lindesnæs in Norway – always purchased that salt in 100 chests – that is, of the so-called *slaplagens chests*, each one holding a good *tønde*, each chest costing 4 marks Danish, and sold some of it later on St. Thomæ Island in West India. Some was also transported to Denmark.[78]

They are mistaken who write that at Labade and other places in Akra, salt is produced by cooking. This is absolutely unnecessary since the sun produces salt so quickly from sea water. When it has been high tide and the surf, during the night, has flooded the flat, clay ground which lies only a stone's throw from the sea, by next midday the flat is completely covered by what resembles thin hoar frost, which is as fine and sharp as the best Lyneborger salt in Europe.

To continue about the people, and especially about the Akra inhabitants: they are indeed a healthy and well-built people, but not nearly as stout, tall and quick, in general, as the people below [to the east]. I am not here speaking of //**128**// one or another single person, who might be the exception, since I have seen Akras who have, indeed, been big and tall.

Their way of living is like that of all the other heathens there, that instead of marriage they take as many women as opportunity provides, and for a man to have 24, even 30, and more is not unusual. I knew [for

---

77  *Pankis* is derived from the Dutch *pantjes*, waist cloth or loin cloth.

78  *Slaplagen* probably from German *Schlaff-Laken*, bed sheet. 1 *tønde* = 144 *potter*, or 139.39 litres.

example] a single, average *kabuseer* who had more than 60 children with 43 women. Indeed, the king of Aqvambu has over 100, and the king of Fida is said to have 500 women. Thus is God's holy establishment perverted in an ungodly manner to an animal-like behaviour.

It costs the men absolutely nothing to support the women; on the contrary, they [the women] compete among themselves to see who can present the man daily with the most wonderful food and nourishment, so that they can gain his favour and confidence.

If a man loses his women or children by their being captured in war, he usually ransoms them, if he can afford it at all. And if a women violates her contract with a stranger, //**129**// or if an inherited slave, who is usually not sold by his master, transgresses with his master's wife, [the master] can freely sell both the woman and the inherited slave.

There is an old superstition among the Blacks that when a slave-owner has sold an inherited slave, and that same slave can approach close enough to his former owner to strike him with a handful of salt, the latter must free him and pay him 4 *benda* or 128 rigsdaler specie, because they are convinced that they would otherwise no longer be able to have any luck or fortune in this world.

But if it is a free Negro who has transgressed with the woman, he has to pay the woman's husband as many *bendas* of gold, to the value that her husband demands of him. This is an accepted right among them, which is not written down in, as it is among us. Nor is it brought to a proper court, where the decision would be carried out; yet it is honoured without argument, unless the man himself waives his right.

As regards the female sex, among the Akraish and Aqvambuish women I have //**130**// not seen, anywhere on the Gold Coast, such ugly, extraordinarily hanging breasts as Dapper describes, apart from 2 or 3 at Del Mina. But in general they have well-shaped, moderately hanging breasts. When the breasts of the young Akraish girls begin to grow they put cups over the outermost part, and let that part, after some time, be pulled out with the cups, like a little ball outside the proper breast, so that it looks like they have double breasts. This is considered to be an especially fine decoration, and those on whom this is most noticeable are considered to be the most beautiful.

# Chapter Fourteen

The women in that country give birth to very small babies, noticeably smaller than newborns in Europe. And when they are newborn they are almost half white, yet mostly brownish red; but they are then smeared with palm oil or tallow into which has been mixed coal or soot. They are then laid in the sun so that, after some 14 days, they have become raven black. Which would have happened without their being smeared. Negroes, or the Blacks, cannot give birth to white children, wherever in the world they live, so the blackness of their skin does not come from the great heat of the sun. //**131**//

I shall not attempt to examine nature's reason for this, as it has been discussed, at times, in detail. But if a *Castits* – one whose father is white and whose mother is a Mulatto – also called *Mistits* – or of a White and a Black, and gives birth to a child with a white person, it is as beautiful as any European child. I have seen examples at Capo Corso [Cape Coast]. In the month of October, 1712, [I saw] 2 little girls whom the sub-agent had bred with a Castits. One of these small girls may have been 11, and the other about 8 years old, and they were so beautiful, white and well-shaped – although they had, in the way of the Negroes, never been either in swaddling or a crib – as if they had been born in London of the oldest English ancestry. This, although their great-grandmother, who was still alive, was an extremely aged Negress and absolutely raven black.

It might indeed be possible, as an Englishman assured me, that a child born of a white father and a black mother is whiter than one who is born of a black father and a white mother. I have, since then, known a person by the name of //**132**// Verville, who was studying in Kjøbenhavn, whose father was Mr. Frideric Rostgaard and his mother a *Morinde* [Moor] or Black. His skin was somewhat dark, but like many who are born of a white mother and father might be just as dark, and those who did not know his origin would not be able to guess it.

Further, I have been told by my now-deceased predecessor, Mr. Andreas Vinter, that [in the case of] those Negroes who in the so-called 'Lygaard's War' had been killed by the Aqvambues on the beach close under the fortress, after they had been lying there for a few days' time, being washed as the surf went in and out, their skin had become pale white.

I have just written that the newborn babies among the Blacks are brownish-red and become coal-black later, yet there are those among them who remain brownish-red all their lives, but they are not considered to be as beautiful as those who are truly pitch- and coal-black.

The women handle childbirth right deftly, since they give birth to the child the one day, and are usually recovered and well again the next day, and do their work //**133**// and carry on their business as if nothing had harmed them. It is almost as if God's judgement – *Gen: 3.10* – had never touched them, or that it had passed by them.[79]

The children are never put into swaddling or cloth, since, because their parents use no clothing the children need it even less. They are never laid in a crib, since no one in that country knows of such things, but when the mother is going to grind millet – which is the foremost business of the women – she binds the *pankis*, or cloth that she wears around her waist so high that it goes around the waist of the child. Then the poor child lies on the mother's back and sleeps while she grinds her millie. If she has some other varying chores that require her to run from one place to another, she lays the child on the ground on a small pillow, and goes about her work, as if the child did not exist or as if nothing could happen to it.

They carry their children either astride their backs, with the child's arms under their arms, or the child is placed under their left arm, as if

---

79  King James version: *Genesis 3:16* '...in sorrow thou shalt bring forth children'. Norwegian 1915 edition: *Genesis* 3:16, '...in pain shall you bring forth your children'.

riding //**134**// on their hip, carrying them thus. However, the latter method is used only for female children.

When a child is born they immediately bind several layers of ordinary glass beads, along with mussel shells, teeth and other rubbish, in the manner of a cross, around the child's neck and under its arms, ostensibly to protect the child from disease and plague.

The Akras circumcise all their male children when they are about 6 or 7 years old, which is also the practice among the Krepees and Fidas. It is unavoidable that you conclude that this could be a remnant of the old Israelites' religion, since they, too, consider circumcision to be holy, in their way, and absolutely necessary. But since there is such great difference between the time of circumcision among the Jews and these heathens, it is more likely that the latter have learnt this directly from Mahumetans, although the Turks, or Muhametans, as well as all heathens who practise circumcision, have originally learnt it from God's establishment for Abraham, and it originates with him.

# Chapter Fifteen

Male and female children all go around totally naked until they are 10 years //**135**// old, and even later. Yet the Akras are more modest than the inhabitants of Qvita [Keta], where the women, whether they are pregnant or not, usually go around naked without shame.

Women in Akra are unwilling to marry any uncircumcised man, although they know nothing of the significance of circumcision, its relationship or advantage, or of its use in any way. Nor are they taught, or care, about it; yet an uncircumcised man is nearly an abomination in their eyes.

Men and women in Akra usually go around naked, with only a strip of linen or wool – called a *pankis* in their language – wrapped loosely around their waist from the belt area and down, in the manner described earlier.[80]

Men have their hair shaved in various ways, which is done with an ordinary knife that is sharpened, since they know nothing of razors. Women have their hair shaved, but not at the top of the crown, where they smear it daily and let it grow long, wind //**136**// it up daily into a round crown, or bun, on top of the head, and bind a row of ordinary glass beads around it. But the whores of the Whites – there are those here who do not deserve to be called Christian, but are distinct from the heathens purely in skin colour, since they misuse many women whom they keep for the same purpose as do the Blacks – these women

---

80 Actually, *pankis* is not a term in the local language, but the Dutch term used by the Europeans. In Ga the large cloth is called *mamma ni le*; the loincloth is called *tɛklɛ* (p.c. Leone de Graft).

bind their hair up in remarkable figures, and fasten the hair here and there with small gold pieces, beads and *agri*.

And now I must tell what an *agri* is. There are those who claim that they are a type of bead which can be described as having various colours. But the Negroes in the kingdom of Harder are unanimous in claiming that *agri* is found in the earth, and since *agri* chiefly comes from there, it seems to be reasonable that it is a kind of marble.[81] It is very hard and the colour is, in some, absolutely blue, and in some very yellow with many black and white veins and marks in them. It is certain that they are found naturally in the earth in the kingdom of Harder, and are sold all over the Coast at equally high prices as gold, especially the latter //**137**// variety, which is considered to be of higher value than gold.

Around the belt area the women bind their *pankis* with a blue or red cloth scarf, on each side of which hang several large bundles of aromatic roots, and among them a small horn full of civet. In the middle of the back hangs, in a chain, a little bunch of small keys or locks made of silver or brass. Bells, as Dapper reports, were formerly much in use among the women on the Gold Coast, but now they are out of fashion, and one hardly sees any old woman wearing them, much less the young. Since they are a haughty people, which sin I have earlier applied to the Blacks, and have had no reason to change my opinion, they are always of unstable mind , subsequently fickle in habits, customs and clothing.

Among other hair ornaments the women on the Gold Coast use some small bone combs with 3 or 4 teeth in them, each tooth a good inch long. This comb, as a sign of respect, is lifted out of their hair arrangement [as a greeting], as we do with our hats //**138**// when we greet someone. I shall not here describe further their business, customs and decorations, since Dapper and others have described in detail all that can be said further about such things.

Males who are wealthy and can afford it also wear many *agris* in their hair, although they do not have longer hair than a month-old black, curly lamb would have of wool, to which I can most easily compare

---

81   R. is referring to Allada in former Dahomey. For description and possible origin of
     aggrey beads see John Fage 'Some remarks on beads..' 343-7; *idem* 'More about aggrey.'
     209-10; Milan Kalous 'Akorite' 203-17.

it, since their hair is that curly; and men do not wear their hair long at any time.

One certainly sees *kabuseer* who, when properly ornamented, wear great, thick gold chains around their neck, rows of pure gold and *agris* around their waist, and gold pieces right down on their legs @ – even on their ankles – which are larger than a ducat. But in all this there is not to be found anything properly fashioned or decorated, according to our tastes.

# Chapter Sixteen

The Blacks can be divided into 4 classes: 1. the inland Negroes, who can be compared to our farmers; 2. *kabuseer,* who can, most conveniently, be compared to our counts and nobility in Denmark; 3. *mercadorer,* who //**139**// are their merchants, or, rather, brokers, since they accompany the inland Negroes to the fortresses, arrange and conclude sales for them, and interpret their language, since those from inland do not understand the Portuguese language, and the Europeans do not understand them; 4. *remidors,* who are, in a sense, their marine folk, knowledgeable about canoes and fishing. Some of them have expertise in rowing [*i.e.* paddling] in and out of the surf, which is the great surge the sea makes toward land. That surge is unbelievably strong, by which we are seriously plagued all along the Coast, and in which many Christians have drowned there. This great and heavy surf is natural there because of the enormous size of the sea off the coast, so its movement cannot but be other than even stronger; and it is characterized by so much fearful noise and roaring where the land receives this violent movement. In this surf the *remidors* know from experience how to find the right condition to be able to steer their canoes unharmed. But when even those canoes are awash, or crushed, they are in no danger because they can all swim like dogs, and use their arms in swimming, in precisely the same //**140**// way a dog uses his forepaws when he is swimming.

The Negroes, show great solidarity among themselves, and are very good to one another; and I have often noticed that no matter how little one gives to them of food or drink, they never fail to share it with their comrades, and they will never enjoy it alone, even if the other one could not see that he had been given anything.

They are, by nature, very foolish, cowardly and easily distracted, but, when nature is given free rein, they are alert and sharp. Most of them have good abilities and quick minds when it comes to learning a number of languages, such as Dutch, English, Danish – with the greatest difficulty – French, Portuguese and all manner of Negro languages, which are countless, and often very different from one another. And, if they are driven to it, or even decide to work themselves, which is much against their inclination, they could be found to be suited to learning all manner of crafts.

The people there are without a flaw in body and limbs, which, according to our conviction of the necessity of swaddling babies, must seem almost unbelievable; but I cannot remember ever seeing anyone who was deformed or with //**141**// crooked limbs, such as are found in great numbers among us, despite all our care and careful swaddling of babies. Thus, I have concluded that the parents make an end of, and dispose of, those children who have some flaw or anything lacking in body or limbs, and only raise those who are flawless. But I never had an opportunity to ask about this, so this is only my own very logical conclusion.

They are sound and healthy and live long, although their food is truly poor, but what I think prolongs their lives is that they are always in good spirits and laughing, never in despair or ever worried about anything; and thus they preserve their spirit, and their bodies are not overworked either, since they take both their sorrow and their work in the easiest way possible, this remarkable folk.

Their sins are many, as can be expected of heathens, but drink, prostitution, thievery and deceit are found alike in both sexes – as well as the faults and sins into which individuals have fallen due to evil customs.

Bodily weakness is found among them, at times, //**142**// but no lameness, deafness, blindness or internal illnesses are found in as great numbers as they are among us. They have no knowledge of internal medicine, as far as I have experienced, although I know that they have, and use, a number of herbs and roots on one or another occasion.

Among other [plants] there are quantities of a kind of nut, as large as an ordinary hazel nut but with much thinner shell. They do not grow on trees but on long vines that run up along fences and poles. If you eat only 2 of these nut kernels you have a perfect laxative of 8 seats.

On this subject I must report an incident that a number of our people have told me had actually happened in their time. A Portuguese sailor who had come from Brazil, once went ashore from his ship that lay in the Christiansborg road. When he came to the people on watch one of their boys had come from the fields and brought his master a half *snes* or more of such //**143**// nuts, for which, possibly, a couple of them had need, since he was weak.[82] When the Portuguese sailor heard what they could be used for he asked for some of them, whereupon our man took a couple himself and gave all the rest to the Portuguese sailor, since enough of them grow everywhere and everyone knows how they work. When the sailor, who had not tasted them before, put the first one in his mouth and found that the kernel tasted sweet and good, he kept on eating them as he stood talking to our people, unconsciously taking one after the other, until he had finished them all. Then he went aboard again immediately, and a couple of hours after that – as he told it later – they began to work so violently, and continued for such a long time that the man was in the greatest danger, and he could not stop it. Finally it stopped, and the sailor was quite well after that. Several days later he came ashore again and told what had happened to him, and was grateful to our soldier for the wonderful cure he had given him, and admitted that he had had a strong attack of *fransoser*, but that, by this //**144**// remedy, he was quit that evil, and found himself as well afterward as anyone would wish to be.[83]

Otherwise, they know more about how to help themselves against *fransoser* or pox than against scabies and rash. Against pox and *fransoser* they know no better remedy than a decoction of sarsaparilla, which they usually take, if it can be found on the ships. The Portuguese must have been the first to acquaint them with that remedy, since it is known to almost everyone that they will not take readily to the Christians' cures unless they are absolutely certain that they are effective, and then only if they know the doctor as a friend.

---

82 *Snes* is a score (20).

83 *Fransoser* means yaws. See Isert (1788/1992) 144 n.73; *idem* (2007) 192 n.73.

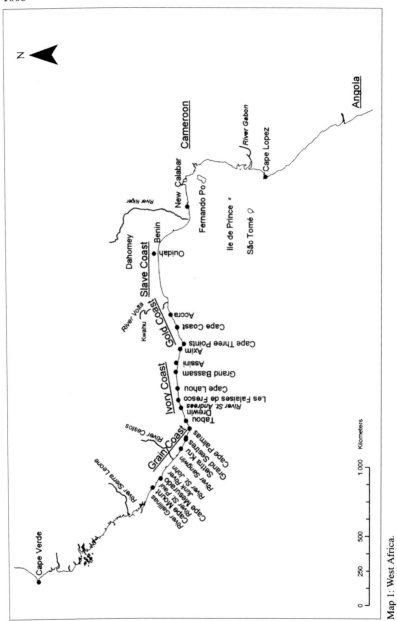

Map 1: West Africa.

*Map of West Africa from Ole Justesen, ed.*
*Danish Sources for the History of Ghana Vol.2, p.1008*

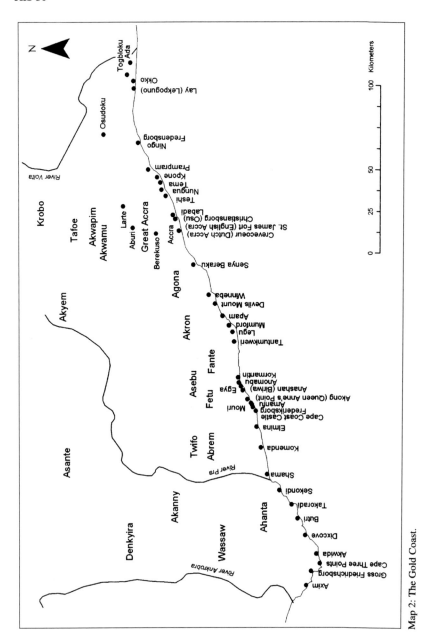

*Map of The Gold Coast ibid. p.1009*

Map 2: The Gold Coast.

Map Six

*The Expansion of Akwamu 1702 from I.Wilks Akwamu 1640-1750 p.xvii*

Map Seven

*The Expansion of Akwamu 1710 from I.Wilks Akwamu 1640-1750 p.xvii*

*Drawing of Christiansborg Castle from L. Svalesen The Slave Ship Fredensborg p. 66*
*Courtesy of the Royal Danish Library, Copenhagen*

*Painting of ships in the Christiansborg roads from L.Svalesen The Slave Ship Fredensborg p. 62*
*Courtesy of The Danish Maritime Museum, Kronborg*

*The keys to Christiansborg Castle from A.A.Y. Kyerematen Panoply of Ghana p. 47*

When they have a headache they mix grated *malaget* [pepper] with water or lemon juice, or with brandy, and rub this over their heads, on their necks and faces. If that does not help they make a cut on their foreheads or on their necks, so that blood runs out. Then they smear *malaget* into the sore, thereby they are relieved. They use the same method for back pain or in whatever limb they feel pain.

//145// They know very well how, very quickly, to heal external sores – from a cut or being pierced – better than our best doctors with all their expertise, if the injured one is not too badly hurt. And truly, it would be a very serious wound before they would not be able to heal it, and do it so well, as I have often seen with wonder. They moisten the wound daily with water, but preferably with palm wine, if the injured person can tolerate it, and put that into the sore; they then dip a wick of linen fibre into the palm oil and put that on the sore. After that they rub all around the sore very well with that same oil, bind a cloth around it, and it does not take a long time before it is quite healed. Thus I have mused, when picturing our apothecaries in Europe – filled with countless beakers and glasses, boxes and bottles, from floor to ceiling; and thinking of the numerous saws, knives, stilettoes, scissors, forceps, awls with which our surgeons load their chests and cupboards – things of which the Negroes know nothing and have not even heard of them, yet they are much better suited than we are, as regards their health care.

//146// Their most serious plague is the so-called worm, which has been described earlier. I have seen many truly cursed by this evil. They call it worm, although it is hardly actually that, in truth, but only because it resembles a white worm. At times it is more than 2 *alen* long, yet not thicker than an ordinary sewing thread. But I have never noticed, nor heard from other reliable people, that there is any life-like movement or any recognizable head on it; and I have observed it very carefully because I concluded privately that it was most unlikely that there could be any place for such breeding so deep in the flesh of the limbs. The infected person feels great pain as far up into his flesh as the worm reaches; and such a worm, with much care, is wound up, little by little, daily, on a stick or a piece of paper, so that it will not be broken off – since, if it is broken off, it then causes the sick person fearful and long-lasting pain, discharging daily much putrid matter. Neither all the Blacks nor all the Whites suffer from this, but [suffering] is mostly due to the latter condition. //**147**// This plague is extremely bad, it causes pain for as long as it lasts, which can be for several weeks. Yet I must say that it can, with reason, be called a benefit since, whether it is a Christian or a heathen, if he has that plague once a year, he is then usually free that year of other weaknesses. In those places where this plague is not found, the Christians, especially are rarely healthy internally.

I saw a particular example in February or March 1713, when I was under way from Barbados to Europe, by way of England. There was a person, by the name of Jppe [?Jeppe] Olivier, born in Harlingen in Frisland. This man had been in service for an assistant-merchant for 8 years at the Brandenborger chief fort, Great Fredericsberg, which is on Capo Tres Puntas. He had, during all that time, been free of weakness, nor did he have that illness during the 9 weeks and more while he and I together stayed at the same hostel in St. Michael on that same island. But 6 to 8 days after we left there, he was //**148**// attacked by this plague, and went around in great pain until 2 days before we sighted the island of Silli, or Sorlings – lying on the western side when going up The Channel – when that plague suddenly stopped.

I do not know any natural causes for this illness, unless it be poor food, and especially the unclean water found there, in which, perhaps, this grows in the body, and then breaks out as swelling, and forces itself through the skin. For this reason both Christians and heathens, who share the inconvenience of that water, all succumb to this plague.

The most difficult and most common weakness for the Christians in that country is high fever, as well as the red and white diarrhea, of which the white is the worst. To treat that illness, both the white and the red diarrhea, they know of no other treatment than, when one has had wind for 2 days, on the 3$^{rd}$ or 4$^{th}$ day at the latest, they use a good purgative, and when that has worked, one takes, every evening, 1 *lod pulv. dysent* dissolved in water, or beer. And sometimes laudanum is used; gunpowder the size of a peppercorn, //**149**// or 8 drops of laudanum liquid.[84] This both calms the diarrhea and pain, results in [internal] calm, which is, otherwise, very rare in this illness. [The internal upheaval] causes the greatest misery that, in that country, carries with it an unbearable weariness and pain in the stomach and abdomen. There is hope of recovering from that illness, no matter how painful it is, as long as no fever appears. But if he contracts that, there is no hope at all, and he can scarcely escape death.

When an Akra dies, the deceased, according to his fortune, is given some gold to take with him in his grave, nor do his surviving friends neglect to give him a *pankis* to have with him, so that wherever he rises again he will not arise naked or poor. This is because they think that he either rises among the Whites in our country – and they have noticed that nakedness is held to be shameful among us – or at any other place on the Coast.

The Aqvambues knew about this habit among the Akras during the war that had been waged just before I arrived there, and knew how to make use of it. Therefore they dug up and rummaged around in all the houses where they knew some *kabuseers* had //**150**// lived a long time ago, to see if they could find any treasure, since the most prominent among them were usually buried in their own houses.

---

84 Laudanum meant a variety of preparations, of which the main ingredient was opium.

# Chapter Seventeen

Akra was formerly a small kingdom itself, but a few years ago the Aqvambues, who live inland, north and northwest of Christiansborg, totally subjugated them. Dapper ascribes to every kingdom in Guinea, especially on the Gold Coast, a size of 8 or 10 miles, and this is, to a degree, correct. But the Aqvambu kingdom is more than 12 miles wide and 24 miles long, since it now has not only subjugated the little kingdom, Aqvahu, but even Akra, where, as far as I know, it comprises the *negeri* lying under Crevecoeur, called Akra; the one under Christiansborg called Ursu; as well as Labbade, Tesse, Abece, Little Nungo, Great Nungo, Temma, Lahi, Punni, and more.[85]

When the Aqvambus want to make a united front, they number 10,000 men and more. And, although they are only vassals of the Akanists [Akim], from whose land //**151**// the gold evidently comes, as reported earlier, and the Akanists are more than twice as powerful as they, yet the Aqvambus, when they wish to, can block the way for them, and prevent their being able to come out of the their country [and go] down to the forts to trade – meaning, here, the forts that are in Akra. But things are not easier for them above Akra either, since all the nations out to the seashore above them, right up to Ankoper, which is more than 50 miles, do the same; and will not allow them free passage to trade down at the forts or the ships. By this procedure they acquire most of the gold that they bring down with them.

Aqvambu has never been subjugated by the Akanists, but, according to the Negroes' own reports, the Aqvambus were, in earlier times,

---

85  For a detailed history of the rise of the Akwamu State see Erik Tilleman *A Short and Simple Account of the Country Guinea* ..(*1697*) 1994, Ch. Seven; Ivor Wilks *Akwamu 1640-1750* , Part Two, Chapters 1 and 2. See also the map showing the Akwamu empire.

refugees, so the Akanists took the opportunity of occupying a section of their land to live on. They had absolutely no status until, because of the harshness of the Akra king towards his subjects, a number of Akras were tempted and bribed to deliver that king into their hands. When they then increased in number, and as merchants and //**152**// warlike people – in which two characteristics they greatly surpassed the Akanists – they embarked on expansion, occupying the land that is now called Aqvambu, where they had gold mines; and since the Akanists are very simple and stupid – and it is certain that they see no farther than what is right in front of them – a short time later, at the defeat of the above-mentioned Akras, they [*i.e.*Aquambus] had gained such great power that the Akanists had just as much, even more, to fear from them than from the Akanists [*sic*]; and then even so much more, since the Aqvambus had also subjugated the Aqvahus. This took place during my time there, in May 1710.[86] However, for the sake of trade, and the great profit and advantage which they can gain from the Akanists, the Aqvambus and all the kings all along the Gold Coast, trade with them, just as a wise owner trades with a good milk-cow which produces generously.

In their customs and well as their clothing and many other ways, the Akras and Aqvambus resemble each other. But if the Aqvambus know how to manipulate the Akanists, so do the Akras, no less, know how to do the same to the Aqvambus, //**153**// when [the Akras] go to the forts or the ships as interpreters to carry on trade, and as brokers for them. As noted above, the men and women in Aqvambu dress similarly to the Akras, but the Aqvambu women have some special ways of dressing their hair. Some dress it so it looks like old-fashioned Danish visor caps. Others shave it off only on the forehead, but on the sides and the top of the head they clip only the ends off and let [the hair] in the back of the head grow as long as it can, which they can then plait beautifully, and set it up in various arrangements.

There, as well as along the entire Coast, the men always go bareheaded. Some of the great *kabuseers* use old hats that have been discarded by the Christians, and that the Whites give them as gifts. If

86  *Ibid.* 34.

there are no silver or gold ribbons on them they themselves add red, blue or white strips of woollen cloth as trimming, and think they are very fine.

I shall not write of the female sex, since they never have anything on their heads, apart from what Nature has given them, which they shave and clip in various ways, as noted above.

Finally, I must fulfil my promise to //**154**// tell about how they handle millie, which is the business of the women. [This is done] without great knowledge and many special tools, as is the case with all their activities. The millie is grated thus. They take a good, large stone, mostly the size of a grown man, that has a somewhat flat side. They lay this with the flat side up, spread over it the millie, which has been softened in cold water. With another round, oblong stone, like a hand stone, and with bodies bent down to earth, they push and rub the millie with both hands until it becomes as fine as they want it, just like a painter grinds his colours. And this is the entire process of preparing their millie. Then they are satisfied with whatever Nature provides for them without any complicated preparation, wherever it is available. And they can provide themselves with what is necessary, and never worry any further, so that their tools are only very few.

# Chapter Eighteen

Now I return to my diary and shall write down, every day, what happened daily during the year **1710**.

In that year, on 13 January, there came to Christiansborg Castle, //**155**// 3 poor and badly manhandled Englishmen, of whom one was completely naked, just as he had come into the world. The other 2 had been stripped to their shirts by French pirates, of whom they reported that there were 5 on the Coast, and 2 of them had recently seized 4 English ships. And these miserable men could not stop complaining about their truly inhuman, harsh treatment.

On the same day there came to the roads a Dutch interloper from Seeland, that had been away from Holland for 8 months, and intended to go straight home, since the French were so strong there at that time.

The next day, the 14th, Aqvando, the King of Aqvambu, sent a messenger to the governor at Christiansborg, asking if he could provide som 1,000 pounds of gunpowder, since [the king] intended, in 3 or 4 days, to go to war against his enemies, the Qvahus and their helpers and allies.

On the 20th of the same month, there came to the road at Christiansborg an English ship with 44 cannons, that exercised extreme care //**156**// because of the great power the French had on the seas. She weighed anchor the same evening and sailed down the Coast.

On the following day, the 21st, I received a letter from our Chief Assistant, Mr. Rost, written on the 16th, reporting that the Aqvahus, at the beginning of that same month, had in effect destroyed a *negeri*, called Kobang, that belonged to the Aqvambus. This had, evidently, angered Aqvando, the King of Aqvambu, sufficiently to force upon the

Aqvahus a war that was hopeless for them, and they were subjugated.

On the next day, the 22$^{nd}$, in the evening, a tiger-animal attacked a Negro in the Dutch *negeri* Akra, and was in the act of dragging away the prey, but others came to his assistance, so that, after a great struggle, he was saved, although he had been badly injured by bites everywhere [on his body].

On the same day there came to the fortress a great *kabuseer* from Akwambu, with an important errand. We noticed that he considered the nails on his right hand to be his fetis, or the sign of his faith, so that he always allowed those nails to grow. They had a curved growth and extended //157// as far beyond his fingertips as anyone else's nail extended from the root to the fingertip. Should anyone remark that work would prevent such long growth, it should be noted that the work done by this kind of person is no more than to eat, drink, play and sleep, [all of which] do not wear down the nails very much. I do not know how strong the arms of these *kabuseers* are, but it would not be advisable to come into conflict with them, unless one has the same trust in his [own] nails as this one does in his.

In the following month, on 13 February, we noticed a particularly large eclipse of the moon at 10 o'clock in the evening. It seemed to be a considerable eclipse to us, but no matter how large or how noticeable it was, the Negroes paid no attention to it, and, when I asked one or another of them about it, they wondered that anyone wanted to look at what they considered to be no more than a cloud crossing the moon.

Early on the morning of 14 March the Negroes came upon a bush dog, a little way east of the fortress, at the end of the lagoon. What he had eaten could not be known, but he lay there half alive //158// until midday, when the governor and I went down to see it. It was only young, not yet fully grown, but was the size of a 6-weeks old calf. Otherwise, they are found, as fully grown, as large as a year-old heifer, with unbelievably strong and thick limbs. Their fur is grey with round black marks as large as a 2-mark piece. In appearance, as regards their body, they resemble a wolf, for which reason many consider them to be a variety of Guinean wolf, as noted above. But as for their legs, they very closely resemble those of the largest variety of English dogs. They do not have sharp claws, like a wolf, but quite natural dog paws. In the skull, however, and in their teeth, with which they are especially well-provided, they are not unlike bears, and, according to what the Negroes say, they act in the same way as bears by standing on their hind legs against whomever is threatening them. But they run on 4 feet, and are not more fleet than a heavy dog, so that by Nature they are better equipped to defend themselves by their large size than by their running speed. Their tongue is as rough in every way as an ox tongue. On the whole, //**159**// they look most like a dog, for which reason they have been given that name.

On 7 April we received, from Qvita, among other things, the largest elephant tusk that I have ever seen in all my life, and others agreed. It weighed 138 pounds, from which one can reasonably imagine the size of the animal that had borne it.

On the 11<sup>th</sup> of the same month, a little past midday, there died at Christiansborg – divinely prepared and spiritually professing in Christ – one of our people, Lance-Corporal Henrik Pedersøn. He was born of well-known middle-class parents in Sarkjøbing in Laaland, who, although they had not been absolutely satisfied that he ventured so far from the country, let him go; and [as I heard] his most painful, heartfelt utterings, I wished that all reckless children who intend to go against the advice of their parents could have heard his pitiful complaint, and seen his intense weeping, as he asked his forgiveness from God; and did not hesitate to ask me if I would assure him that God would show him mercy for that sin? Yet, what was foremost in his mind was that //**160**// his sin against his parents would continue long after this when they, heartbroken, were informed of his death. Therefore, he asked that I would read certain sections of the gospel – in which he was, for his young age, very well versed – and that I would include, for him, not just the usual Word of God, which promises to every penitent forgiveness for all their sins by the extreme sacrifice by Christus, but also especially those [prayers] in which Christus declares His obedience to His Father until His death on the cross: *Phil: 2.8.*; his humility towards his parents: *Luc: 2.51*; his concern for his mother, even on the cross: *Joh: 19.26*. Having received that complete forgiveness granted to all disobedient but repentant and contrite children, this finally so convinced him that, full of comfort and hope, he entrusted his soul to the crucified Christ. He had not been at the fortress longer than one year, less 5 days, and his condition was not otherwise than that there was a good chance he would come home, to the joy of his parents, had God spared him his life.

//**161**// On 11 June a Negro brought a snake into the fortress, one that he had killed in the fields. It was twice as large as the one we beat to death in our warehouse on 31 May 1709. It was just a young one of the largest variety of snakes that, when they are fully grown are 6 fathoms long.

A few years ago one of our people had shot one of the same variety, and found inside of it a fully grown deer. Several of our people could bear witness to this, which cannot be so unbelievable when one considers that the small snakes in our country can swallow a whole mouse, which is sometimes found inside of them and it makes us wonder how they can kill them.

I saw the skin of such a snake, stuffed, in October 1712, hanging under the beams in the long hall at the Brandenborg fortress, Frideriksberg, at Capo Tres Puntas. Further, on the breastwork of Christiansborg, I once saw a snake that was almost 2 *alen* long, and thick as a good-sized thumb. It was very green, and as clear and transparent as glass. I made off after it as best I could, but //**162**// it slipped into a crack in the wall, so I saw it no more; but according to the testimony of other people, it must have been of the variety that is the most poisonous.

On 20th of the same month one of the soldiers, by the name of Maurits Jessen, when he had gone out hunting, had caught a small, young crocodile that was about one and one-half quarters [?*alen*] long. It had a double sting [*sic*] and could use its 4 legs very forcibly.

The following month was strange because on 3 July Aqvando, the King of Aqvambu, came home from the Qvahu war, having won a total victory – in which the Aqvambus certainly did their part, although others had done just as much as they to assure a favourable outcome.

On 1 August we sought information from a skipper who had come to the Christiansborg road a couple of days earlier on an English newspaper sloop [*sic*] from Barbados. On the 12 and 13 March before

this date the ship had been in the St. Thomae road in West India –
on which island the Danish fortress Christiansfort lies, but he had not
seen the Danish Guinea sailer that //**163**// had sailed there from the
Coast the year before, in September; nor had he seen any Danish ship.
This report saddened us seriously, since the best time for loading and
sailing from there is usually in the middle of April.

On 4th of the same month, in the evening, our drum major, Christian
With, shot a Guinean stork at the lagoon under the fortress. It was just
as long-legged as those in Denmark, but not so agile and large in body.
In walking, feathers and appearance it was like ours, apart from the
beak, that was somewhat larger than ours, indeed twice as large, and in
the part where the beaks of our storks are red, these were yellow and
hard as carved ivory, and from the uppermost end of the back right up
to the head the skin was bare and resembled red parchment.

Later, on 19th of the same month, I saw how the *remidors* at Ursou –
the *negeri* that lies directly under the gate of Christiansborg – who are
usually fishermen, made an offering to their sea-god, so that he would
give them plenty of fish and good weather. Precisely at the place where
they drag their boats and canoes up when they //**164**// come ashore,
lying close under the fortress, there is a very large, flat stone on which
they had placed some other stones. It is covered with seaweed, as the
stones on the cliffs by the sea usually are. These stones are their *fitis*, or
god. Onto that stone they pour beer, brandy, cooked millie porridge
and palm oil: this is called *kabuseer canchis,* that is 'master-porridge'.
They have built a hut of leaves over that stone, convincing themselves,
in their remarkable blindness, that when they have aroused their *fitis*,
or god, to whom they had given no refreshment for 2 years, he would
give them plenty of fish. With what thanks can we repay God for having
revealed Himself to us and cleansed our consciences to serve the living
God.

On 13 September, early in the morning, I became aware, to my
surprise, that a Negress was standing behind the smithy, crying and
talking to herself, and thus making her weekly sacrifice at the spot
where the Aqvambus, in the last war, had decapitated her sister. [I] was
informed by a Mulatto who had been born at the fortress, but //**165**//

was fully knowledgeable about the Negroes' idolatry, that it was the custom among the Akras to offer such sacrifices weekly, on the day of the friend's death, at the site of their death, with some beer or brandy. After she had made her sacrifice to the earth [i.e. poured libation], she remained standing for a little while, cried and talked so softly to herself that I could not understand [what she said].

Sprinkling some of their drink is the Akras' customary manner of showing honour to their *fitis*. It is very strange to see that some Negroes – caring little about what kind of drink they are given – spray the first drops they have taken into their mouths onto their breast, onto the *fitis* bag they usually have hanging around their necks. These are either a small, square piece of hide sewn together, which is, weekly, on the day of their birth, also sprinkled with blood, but it must never be opened. Or, it is a stick bound round with hide, into whose opening there has been bound a small twist of animal fur – like the women's hair *fitis* – [containing] a couple of small red feathers from the tail of a parrot. Or it is a small calabash with //**166**// a solid lump of wax, which also must not be opened, all of which are treated equally with this sprinkling. If they have small *fitis*-tassles or small *fitis* pieces of a piece of animal hide bound into their hair, they also spit a few drops out of their mouths onto their hands, and then stroke it on their heads. Indeed, not even the poorest slave – who cannot pay for this imagined sacred object that is bought from their *fitisiero* for money – before he himself drinks he also spits a few drops out of his mouth onto his breast, or onto a flat spot of earth for the *fitis*, so his drink is then sacred. Yet, this is not done except for the first drink, since once it is done, they then drink abundantly, as much as they can get, sometimes until they can neither see or walk. If it is a palm-wine party, where they fill themselves absolutely without limit – although brandy is the true Negro nectar, and drink of angels – they only honour the *fitis* with the first mouthful, in the manner described above, and then in each kalabash of wine, from which they drink, they leave a little in the bottom, which //**167**// is poured out onto the ground with such force that there is a loud sound and splash on the ground. And the one who pours this shouts, at the same time, *'Majaba!'*, whereupon all the others, as many as there are in the party, also answer with a more powerful voice, *'Majaba!'*[87] And such offerings are meant for the *fitis*, and are poured to show him honour, according to their way of thinking.

In that same year, on 6 October, a comical thing happened when our constable's black Boy was sitting safely out in the forework sunning himself. [Suddenly] he sank into the earth, which terrified the poor heathen, since the earth sank under him. [This was because] at that same place there had been buried, a few years ago, a chief mate by the name of Alexander Danefær, who had come out from Denmark in 1705, with a company ship called *Cron Princen*, and died there. And when the Negro realized it was a grave, he hurried up out of the hole and, as fast as he could, he ran, quite terrified, and bought beer and brandy and made a sacrifice to his *fitis*, pouring it at that same place, and performed this very spiritually, in his own way and according to his forefathers' blindness, so that the *fitis*, which he //**168**// completely convinced himself had summoned him, would let him live a little longer.

On 25 November, which was a Tuesday, that is the weekly holy day for the *fitis*, early in the morning, at sunrise, I saw 2 fishermen in a canoe outside the breakers. They were offering their *sea-fitis* some brandy so that he would grant them a generous catch of fish. When they had drunk to their *fitis* – often pouring the rest into the sea – and given forth a great shriek of joy, the others who were standing on land, displayed their ignorant joy with shrieks of joy and shouting.

---

87 *Majaba* is probably from Ga, *Manye* ( or *Omanye*) *aba*, meaning 'May peace and prosperity come!'(p.c. M.E. Dakubu)

# Chapter Nineteen

The languages in Guinea are very many, but even though each people in that country, live indeed scarcely 1 or one and one-half miles from each other, be they Infanties, Akanies, Akras, Aqvambus, Kræpees, Qvahus, Qvitas, Harders, Popos, Fidas, and I shall not even mention those in areas above [west of] and below [east of] these, each of whom has his own special language that they use among themselves – if Dapper is correct – yet it is the Aqvambuish [i.e. Twi] that is, so to speak, their chief language, in which almost 100 miles above Akra, and nearly as many miles below, they can communicate.

//**169**// I shall record some as a sample of the Aqvambuish language. Aqvambus can count as high as we can, and their numbers are as follows:

| | | | | | |
|---|---|---|---|---|---|
| Biakun or Eko | = | 1 | Eduasung | = | 17 |
| Abien | = | 2 | Eduoqvi | = | 18 |
| Abiesang | = | 3 | Eduaknung | = | 19 |
| Anang | = | 4 | Eduno | = | 20 |
| Anung | = | 5 | Eduafa | = | 30 |
| Asiang | = | 6 | Edunan | = | 40 |
| Asung | = | 7 | Edunung | = | 50 |
| Quqvi | = | 8 | Edusiang | = | 60 |
| Asnung | = | 9 | Edusung | = | 70 |
| Edu | = | 10 | Eduoqvi | = | 80 |
| Edubiakung | = | 11 | Eduknung | = | 90 |
| Eduebin | = | 12 | Aha | = | 100 |
| Edubiesang | = | 13 | Apim | = | 1,000 |
| Eduanang | = | 14 | Apim Edu | = | 10,000 |

| | | | | | |
|---|---|---|---|---|---|
| *Eduanung* | = | 15 | *Apim Aha* | = | 100,000 |
| *Eduasiang* | = | 16 | | | |

And to continue, there now follow other words in their language, just as a small sample from which the rest can be judged. In most of the words the accent usually falls at the end of the word in speech, with very few exceptions. There are also words among them that seem to resemble European //**170**// [words], especially those of the Portuguese, who were the first to sail to this country. As regards letters or script, they know nothing of these themselves.

*Jankumpung* – God

*Safa* – Devil

Angels – they do not know what they are, or how they can be useful; they have no name for them

*Øjia* – Sun

[This term] seems to be the same as 'eye' in their language.

*Esran* – Moon

*Uvami* – Stars

*Adade* – Earth

*Oto aprim* – they shoot with cannons

*Bani* – Man

*Obia* – Woman

*Abafra* – Boy

*Afraba* – Girl

*Mi ba* – My child

*Atja* – Father

*Ona* – Mother

*Akoa* – Slave

*Øjqvia* – Dog

*Porko* – Pig

From this name it appears that they had not seen this kind of creature before the Portuguese had brought them here, just as they do not know about pigs at many other places.

*Pungkao* – Horse

*Nang* – Cow

*Akoko* – Hen/Chicken

*Anoma* – Bird
*Gynsoba*/ Griffelba – oak
*Øsa* – Elephant
*Insumbeng* – Elephant's tusk
**//171//**
*Abohinne* – Tiger
*Tyty* – Bush dog
*Abringpung* – The most prominent man after the king
*Grandi* – sword, sabre
*Etru* – Box
*Atrudu* – Gunpowder
*Abo* – Bullet
*Akungsong* – Ape/Monkey
*Kangkang* – Civet cat
*Ekora* – Nut
*Insu* – Water
*Ariva* – Basin
*Akiørbu* – Flint box
*Papa* – Coarse cloth
*Atinkang* – English bay
*Prammesi* – *Slaplaken*
*Abronsa* – Brandy
*Ahaj* – Beer
*Bolle* – Baked bread
*Kankis* – Steamed bread or porridge
*Abru* – Millie
*Uvisa* – Malaget [pepper]
*Taba* – Tobacco
*Bele* – Tobacco pipe
*Aura* – Sir, Head of the household
*Kakla:* Gakang – Knife
*Ble* – Cloth, Handkerchief
*Akankama* – Small Guinean lemons, usually sold at 10 for 1 skilling
*Abo* – Stone or a ball [?bullet/cannonball]
*Odia* – Fire

*Dango* – House, cottage
*Edung* – clock
*Nam* – Fish
*Inve* – Yes
*Aahaa* – No
*Augua* – Stool
*Afhøve* – Mirror
*Epono* – Table
*Daka* – Rifle
*Epa* – Bed //**172**//
*Taffa ?Tassa* – Tin, or brass basin
*Etiu* – Hat, Cap
*Adebang* – Iron
*Adibang* – Food
*Atumba* – Glass bottle
Candle-light – lamp, undoubtedly from the Portuguese language
*Acin* – vinegar, appears to be from the Dutch language
*Brombadi Nam* – stockfish, dried fish
*Nim* – Face
*Eniba* – Eye
*Toi* – Ear
*Gungo* – Nose
*Onabu* – Mouth
*Efa* – Hand
*Oabi* – Right hand
*Odentin* – Left hand
*Esatiaba* – Fingers
*Akri* – Back
*Unsu* – Stomach
*Tekerna* – Tongue
*Ese* ((Efe)) – Teeth
*Nang* – Legs
*To* – Buttocks
*Ito* – Head
*Aboge* – Beard

*Babi* – Nail

*Ohin* – Forehead

And here are some of their daily expressions on various occasions:

*Bra haj* – Come here

*Im Præ* – Exactly on time

*Teto Aura de* – Excuse me, Sir

*Afena* – Tomorrow

*In de* – Today

*Oba haj Akerre* – Have you been here long? //**173**//

*Gaa faj Odia bra* – Go fetch fire

*Jai a Jankumpung tira* – Be quiet, for God's sake. After the words: Be quiet, by God's head.

The Negroes, as do other people, have personal names, which seem useless to us, yet there are found a multitude of their names which are either the same, or closely resemble, those found in the Scriptures. As proof, here are a few for the reader's consideration:

*Tohi* – seems to be in agreement with Thoi, mentioned in 2 *Sam*: 8.9.

*Aservi* – agrees with Aser, Jacob's son's name. *Gen*: 30.13.

*Cai* – sounds almost like the common name Kæj: Cajus, found in *Rom*: 16.23

*Geravi* – can be compared with Gear, Benjamin's son's name. *Gen*. 46.21

*Bunni* – is the same sound as that mentioned in *Nehem*: 10.15

*Ahimaa* – closely resembles Ahimaaz, a name borne by many, 1 *Sam*: 14.40

*Amma* – agrees very well with Amma, found in 2 Sam: 8.1., that is the name of a city or town. In their language it refers to ground millie. //**174**//

*Quqvi* – is a man's name, but also signifies the number 8, just as we use the name *Otte* [eight] which does not necessarily derive from the Roman Otto, since we use other numbers as names: Ellev [eleven], Tolv [twelve] or Tollev, etc. Furthermore, there was a slave in the service of our Company who was called Octavi. If that was derived from Octavius, I include it.

*Ako* – is very much like our much-used name Aake, Aage or Haagen.

*Adom* – resembles closely the name of the first man, Adam

*Aja* – this name is found in many places in the Scriptures: *Gen.* 36.24; *Sam.* 3.7. Aje is also used as a man's name in many places in Norway.

*Amrama* – sounds precisely like Amram, which was the name of Moses' father. *Exod*: 6.18.

*Amok* – is the same name that is found in *Nehem*; 12.7

*Ammo* – agrees with Ammon, *Gen*: 19.38

*Bani* – a name like this is found frequently in the Scriptures. 2 *Sam*; 23.26; *Nehem*: 3.17. etc. //**175**//

*Buki* – the same name is borne by a nobleman of Dan's clan. *Num*: 34.22, and several others.

*Dodo* – This name has also been borne by several in the Scriptures. 2. *Sam*:23.9, etc.

*Sakei* – closely resembles Sacai. *Nehem*: 7.14; or Zachæus, *Luc*: 19.2

*Davite* is a name used here and is just like David, which, in the Scriptures, is known to all.

*Ahye* – Ahia. 1 *Sam*: 14.3

*Lavie* – Levi. *Gen*: 29.34

*Bus* – Bus. *Gen*: 22.21

*Akante* – Akan. *Josv*: 7.1

*Anane* –Ananias. *Act*: 5.1

*Abihu* – Abihu, Aaron's son. *Exod*: 6

*Abisaio* – Abisai. 1 *Sam*: 26.6

*Age* – Age. 2 *Sam*. 23.11

*Ammon* – Ammon. *Gen*: 19

Thus could many others be reported, but those written above must be enough, since in all languages there are words that seem to be alike, without their either being the same or having been derived from each other. Since the numerous languages did not arise by people travelling here and there of their own volition, who could retain their first language, although with some changes increasing in time, //**176**// but by a just and very severe punishment by God [who caused] languages to become mixed and confused, and they are daily confused more and more, so that it is a great mistake to want to derive the present languages from the Hebraic as the first one. This must now be enough of writing about the Negroes' language, which is of no great consequence.

# Chapter Twenty

Now I turn to other customs they practise, of which the following one is totally heathen. When 2 Negroes are going to wage war together against their enemy, and wish to swear loyalty and fidelity to each other, they each cut themselves with a knife and drink one another's blood.

The Fida Negroes usually cut the most figures in their skin, which they consider to be a special decoration. The flesh that has healed and been covered with scar tissue – found among many of them after deep wounds – is certainly not easily distinguishable from the large cut that they hold to be decorative, since they use small round, or oblong, calabashes instead of cups, to suck the skin into round or oblong //177// figures. [The scar becomes] as thick and large above the flat skin as the joint of a large finger; into which they cut stripes in the length and across, which do not disappear. I shall not speak of other cuts.

Yet they scar mostly those who have become mad, of whom a greater number are found at Fida than anywhere else. And they consider it to be a helpful remedy for disturbance of the mind, which does very often bring them peace of mind again, just as bleeding from the forehead does for us.

It has been noted above that every Tuesday is their weekly holiday or holy day, so they normally know of no other. Yet every *kabuseer* keeps holy that day of the week on which he was born. Then, so as not to contaminate himself, he has nothing to do with women, nor must any woman cook his food or prepare anything for him on that day. He relaxes, and is bathed on that day; and his most prominent Boy – whom he calls *okra* and who is his intercessor – dries him, using the opportunity to wish him well: that he might have many children with his women, that he must live long, that no one might //**178**// hit him with a shot, that no one might cut off his head, and such things, and all such things that are asked of *Jankumpung*, or God.[88]

This *okra*, or guardian-Boy, always accompanies his master wherever he goes, and when the master stands and converses with someone, he usually leans on the Boy's shoulder; and when the master, or *aura*, dances and enjoys himself, the Boy always follows him and holds his arms with both hands. Indeed, when the master is given something to drink, that same *okra*, for the sake of his master's safety, drinks and tastes it first.

These weekly birthday celebrations are sanctified by the *kabuseers*, on that day, by having a sheep or goat slaughtered, or a chicken, and if there is nothing else available, a dog suffices. He smears his stool, his bed, and his *pankis* with the blood of the slaughtered animal. At times he smears himself and his head with it, thus honouring the flesh, using the meat of the dog as well as some other meat without distinction, it is still a great *fetis* and sacred. //**179**// Since I have mentioned the honour that the dogs in Guinea enjoy, that they are eaten as something sacred, I must here describe, in detail, those dogs which, in certain ways, differ from our European dogs. Their bodies are very straight, they are long-legged and with pointed snouts. They are never heard to bark, since they cannot bark any more than the dogs do in Greenland. Therefore, when the Blacks hear any European dog bark, and see that it can perform various tricks that it has learnt – either to dance, or pretend to smoke tobacco, handle a stick like soldiers with their guns, jump over a pole, lie down in one way or another, get up again and bark, etc. according to what he is ordered to do – they display the greatest wonder, and say that the Whites' dogs can speak and understand. Otherwise, the Blacks' dogs are very willing, and are particularly good at hunting; but they are not alert at night, and cannot be used as watchdogs at all, since

---

88  The *okro* represents the soul of the master. For explanations, see A.A.Y.Kyerematen, *Panoply of Ghana* 110; Kofi Asare Opoku *African Traditional Religion*, 26, 94-6.

they, no less than all other animals, must be carefully locked indoors, for fear of wild and ravenous animals.

As regards the usual manner, in that country, //**180**// of greeting one another, I must tell you here, that the customary manner everywhere, when someone, either Christian or heathen, approaches or leaves a Negro, one takes the host's hand 3 times – or usually up near the elbow – and between each handshake one makes an audible click in his own hand with his own finger, and the Negro does the same. But they do not kiss, so you never see them greet one another by kissing.

When a prominent man enters one of their 'caser', or houses, in order to assure [him] that nothing poisonous or injurious or evil will be given to him to drink, there is brought out a reasonably large amount of palm wine or beer in a large calabash, or pot. The host then takes a small calabash full, pours a few drops on the ground, in the manner described above, and then drinks to his guest.

Women, neither wives – if one can use such an honest title – nor the subordinate wives, ever come into the man's rooms unless they are summoned. The men and //**181**// the women have their own separate rooms in the house, where each can always be found separately.

Never must a Negress eat with the men; indeed, they dare not even let the man see that they see him eating at all, since this is considered a far too free contact, in conflict with the respect women are required to show the men.

In like manner, none of the several wives nor mistresses dares to lie with the man at night, or enter his bed, unless he summons her. In certain cases this is necessary because this objectionable license of taking so many women is the practice, since, otherwise, there would be quarrels and conflicts, both orally and physically, in the bedroom.

The Negroes raise many children with their many women. Our Chief-Assistant, Mr. Rost, in the just past month of October, brought with him a Negro's son from Lampe – which lies just below Rio Volta. The boy was to be kept at the fortress as hostage, or security, so that the Company's servants or goods that were down there would not be poorly treated. //**182**// [Mr. Rost] assured me that the boy's father, Sinde by name, had bred a good 200 children with his wives; and in spite of the fact that that same Negro was old and totally grey, he showed the Chief Assistant some 70 children who had been born in the course of 20 years. But that *kabuseer* had some 100 wives.

When two peoples, after having waged war against each other, make peace, they 'eat *fitis*' with each other. The food they eat at that meal is usually water, blood and ground millie, mixed together. This means that if either of them breaks the oath, it will result in death. But I have heard another explanation for this oath, which seems more reasonable to me. Our drum major, Christian Whit, who is a native heathen on his mother's side, and was 30 years old before he was christened by my blessed predecessor, told me: that the water means an unhappy death in the sea or in another water; the blood means a violent death by gunshot or sword, by which his //**183**// blood will be shed; that the millie [signifies] that all the blessings of the earth's fertility will be denied him, if he breaks the oath.

# Chapter Twenty-one

Since I have so often spoken of millie, I hope it will not be displeasing to the reader, who may know nothing about it yet, if I now write a rather detailed description of millie. There are 2 kinds of millie. The largest variety, on which I have found more than 200 grains on a cob, is as large as a fairly large, grey pea in size, and, among the Aqvambues it is reddish, but above Akra, in most places, it is pale yellow. In Akra you find the best millie of the large variety, which I have seen in some places. It is not as large, yet clearer and whiter, and it produces a better bread than that found in other places. It grows like sugar cane, but with a greater distance between each joint, and one can often find 4 millie cobs on one cane, of which 64 can easily produce 1 sack of pure millie. One must profess to honour Nature's mighty masters, creators and regents, that Nature has very neatly and artfully and beautifully dressed this corn, as it sits //184// on the cob, in wide and closely covering leaves all around it. Permitting my thoughts to run free, I consider that one of the places in our Danish Bible, found in 2 Kings:4.42, presented for common knowledge, may have been millie cobs. And with even greater conviction, I do believe that at Akra, and likewise, in other places in eastern countries, where such millie cobs grow annually, that as they take them off the cane in their natural shells, or husks, as gifts to each other [sic], from which millie they immediately remove the husks, and roast them on a stick over a coal fire, and the taste is not unpleasant.

But the worst is that the Akras allow the land to lie unused to such a great extent. In the interior of the country the people are more energetic and industrious, while those at the seaside depend upon their salt and fish, for which they receive plenty of millie from those inland, who need their salt and demand their fish; and so, by working the earth diligently they raise enough millie.

The smaller variety of millie is also planted at Akra, but mostly it is among the Kræpees, the Popos and the Fidas and those //**185**// below, as well as at Great Akra, as it is now called, and is an island that is incomparably fertile, several miles in circumference, in the Volta lagoon. When the Aqvambus conquered old Akra, where Christiansborg is located, most of the Akras, and the best of them, fled to [this island] and settled there. The small millie grows on a stem – like a cattail in Denmark in reed-grown bogs – abundantly on every stem, but each grain is no larger than a good-sized hemp seed. It provides very good bread, and is the same kind as that we here in Europe make of millet grain.

It should be noted that the Negroes do not plough, as we do, but using hoes, they first remove all the bushes and roots from the ground they plan to use. After that they break up the earth with hoes and set the millie, like we do sugar peas; and the small millie is thus very meagre, since the earth is prepared in that manner.

Dapper may, with good reason, say that the greatest part of the earth lies unused and neglected, and I dare say that, were these people as industrious and diligent as they are in these [above-mentioned] kingdoms and countries, one could hardly fine a more fertile //**186**// land in the world than Guinea; especially inland where there is regular rainfall, which is frequently lacking at the coast and thus doing great damage to the earth's produce and fruits.

However, to the Akras' credit it must be said that they would certainly not insult another by taking the neighbour's land or fields; but always, toward the time for sowing – which at Akra is in the month of April, and harvesting is in the month of July – all the people of the village or town gather and confer with one another about which section of earth each wishes to work, and how much each one wishes to cultivate; and without any conflict that section is [agreed to as] his. This is commendable when compared to the Europeans' endless conflicts and arguments about a foot of earth, but this does not result so much from the inhabitants' sense of justice and virtue, as it does from their natural laziness, that they do not demand much earth, since that would require more work.

They have no fences or ditches around their land, but those who have cattle always have one or another of their children or slaves staying with them to guard them; and //187// when the millie is almost ripe, they set up huts among the plants. [These huts] are a stone's throw from each other; they stand on 4 high poles, where there are always, in the daytime, small boys sitting there, who shout, scream and shoot stones by a catapult, like the ones the boys in our country use. [Thus] they chase and frighten the birds away from the fields. But at night the large porcupine, as well as wild boars are in control in the interior of the country; but not at the shore where they cannot stay because of the lack of forest, as well as buffaloes and even elephants, who frequently do great damage to their millie. But everywhere, when the grasshoppers come, that is the worst [that can happen], and more destructive than anything else.

For fertilizer they make use of the ashes that remain in the places where they have burnt off all the bushes that they uproot from the land [to be used] for sowing. These ashes are carefully spread around over the entire area where each one has planned to cultivate millie. This is a strong and good enough fertilizer, as one recognizes from the practice of burning off the fields in places here in Norway, and it produces an abundance of grain.

//188// The Negroes have only one special oath by which to testify, and that happens when they swear by their dead friends. When the say: '*Me tangora mi Ona*', that means 'I swear by my mother!', indicating that she is dead, and that is their chief and inviolable oath. Otherwise, their daily oath is usually on the king's name, which brings to mind a similarity to what is read in the *Scriptures*, not only about Joseph, who swore by pharoah's life, in *Gen.* 42.15.16, but also about Abner in *1 Sam*; 17,55, etc. But such oaths are not used without good grounds.

Cursing is hardly heard among them, and where it is used they probably learned it from the Whites. I must not say 'Christians', since, alas, they often show themselves to be more libidinous and evil than the heathens. Their cursing, when they do curse, is of the sort : *Sasa eduasa teten*, that is '[May] 30 devils tear you to pieces'.[89] But if they do not curse, yet they do not lack even more wicked words, of which one hears far too many.

Since they have no knowledge of script or seals with which to certify their //**189**// oral promises, [this is what they do] instead. When they make a promise, for faithful assurance that it will be kept, they take hold of their beard and beat their chest, which is just as certain as any written word. Because they hold their beards in such high respect, one can, therefore, show a Negro no greater insult, nor one for which he can take greater offence, than if one, in disrespect or anger takes him by the beard.

---

89 *Sasabonsam* is the evil spirit among the Akan. For a description, see Asare Opoku (1978) 72-3.

# Chapter Twenty-two

Their funerals are very heathenish and gruesome, since, when an Aqvambuish *kabuseer* dies, they bury his foremost and most beloved wife, alive, next to him in the grave, either standing or lying down; and she can stand thus for 2 or 3 days before she dies. However, she goes to such a death willingly, indeed, dancing and jumping around to the sound of the hornblowers and drums. As it happened shortly before my time there, if the *kabuseer* who is to be buried is one of particular prominence, which was the case with Ensangdu, the brother of the Aqvambu king, some 100 slaves were beheaded so that, as they explain, he could arrive where he would rise again with an impressive following, according to his station.

When 'custom', as they call it, or funeral, was held for the above-mentioned Ensangdu, //**190**// not only one but several of his wives died in the terrible manner described above, but, in addition, many slaves were beheaded. And since a *kabuseer* himself could not have afforded to provide so many slaves, the other *kabuseers* made contributions. I asked my informers how they had the heart to kill their slaves thus, who had cost them so much and who could serve them far better, to which they answered that for this purpose they used only the old, crippled and weak, so that they would become young and healthy when they rose again.

When this custom is being made over such a powerful *kabuseer* and a Christian comes to observe it, he is given, in preference over any of the friends of the deceased, a sword that resembles a long and wide slaughterer's axe. With this he may behead as many of those who are to be executed as he wishes to, and those who are to die place their head, willingly, on the block, particularly when they are to be beheaded by a White man. For this I can give no other reason than that they imagine that they shall rise again among the Whites, and without //**191**// doubt become as white as the Europeans.

When any Akras die, all their family and close relatives are summoned to grieve over the dead, which is done with a horrible screeching and howling. Then a strong man takes the deceased, who is wrapped in 2 or 3 *pankis*, or cloths, throws him onto his back, and runs around the grave with him, all the while asking the deceased if he wants to be buried. To this, one of the family answers, 'No', on behalf of the deceased. This is done 3 or 4 times. Finally, the person who has been answering on behalf of the deceased answers, 'Now he wants to be buried!', whereupon, enshrouded, as noted above, he is pushed into the hole.

They do not make their graves, as we do, long enough for the deceased to lie in them, but dig only a hole deep enough for the deceased, in an upright position, to be covered with earth. The most prominent among them are buried thus in their own houses, but for the ordinary people there is a special place outside their villages. When this is finished and the deceased is covered with earth, they cry and howl just as pleasantly as before, and then //**192**// continue shooting, drinking and shouting all through the day.

Of the Akras' weekly sacrifice for their deceased relatives who have died a violent death, especially those who have been executed by their enemies, I have described it above on the occasion of that Negress whom I saw on 13 September 1710, enthralled in that unpleasant business.

A thief, especially at Fida, is absolutely in bondage and outlawed, since if he is caught with the least amount of his goods, under the direction of an elder, or the oldest *kabuseer* in the village, he is excommunicated. Then one can, without mercy, either kill him on the spot without appeal, or sell him immediately, if there is no one who wishes to pay a certain price for his release.

If a Negro is in debt to a White or a Black and has neither given *impie*, that is security, or will not agree to repay, [his creditor] can either capture the man himself, or one of his people, and retain them until payment has been made. But if neither he nor any of his people can be caught, then one can take anyone else in the debtor's place, and he, then, must make payment.

//193// Among some of the Guineans it is the custom that if one becomes extremely angry with another and is unable to wreak revenge, he shoots himself to death, or cuts his own throat, placing the blame on his enemy. Then his surviving enemy must die, or pay a ransom for his life as high as the dead man's friends may demand.

Witchcraft, or sorcery, are absolutely unknown to the Negroes, which is the Christians' good fortune; but it is also a great disgrace that those Europeans who have become Christian by having made a pact with God, may become so godless and desperately evil, that they will make a pact with the Devil to do evil, and become worse than the Devil.

If one demands of a Negro who has some wit – of whom there are only a few – that he shall explain his thoughts about heaven and earth, about God and the Devil, he has no other way of explaining himself than that he paints a cross with chalk, or just with his finger, on the ground and pointing to the uppermost end, indicates that God lives there with his wives and children: that those people who are most obedient to Him, He will make them white, let them learn much, and give them the right side of the Cross, where they shall live. But //194// those who are not righteous and good, are given the left side to stay in, and at the lowest end live those who do a great deal of evil and hold with the Devil, and they will live in Hell with the Devil. They refuse to believe that the damned are tortured in Hell, but do say that *Sasa*, or the Devil, is a very disobedient and contrary man against God, and he either entices or steals people from God, to their corruption.

When the Negroes go to war with each other, as soon as a king or *kabuseer* takes another one captive, he promptly has his trustworthy messenger carry the head [of the captive], in a *lakof*, or sack (as described above) to show to his confidential friends, even if they live several miles away. It should also be understood that whoever the king captures, be it a *kabuseer* or a *kabuseer's* slave, or one or another free

Negro, he [the king] receives the prize and whatever follows it, which comprises the wives, children and inherited slaves of the prisoner or the deceased, as his own. If a *kabuseer* falls to a free Negro who is not a *kabuseer* himself, //**195**// he keeps him as a prize himself. However, the victor cannot take over the property of the captive before there is a total victory, which means the death of the king, since, as long as the kings on both sides are alive, victory is not complete.

If a king, *kabuseer*, or free Negro takes an ordinary Negro captive, they do not kill him nor take him into their own service against their enemy, but they sell him. But if it is a king or *kabuseer* who is captured, he is not spared in any way, nor is he sold, but is immediately killed on the spot. If it happens that the king or regent is the first man to fall in battle, both the battle and war come to an end, and his entire kingdom is lost and falls to the victor, including his people and property. But if each one falls or is captured, and the king, alone, remains alive, all the property remains with the living owner, and he is seen to be better than all his subjects.[*sic*] This agrees with what we read in: 2. *Sam*: 18.2. //**196**// This comprises the rights in war, and is held to be inviolable.

# Chapter Twenty-three

Low and high tides do not occur with the same regularity as they do here in Nordland. They are especially irregular during the rainy and *travade* times, which is their winter in Guinea. Then it is as cold as the month of August in Denmark. It begins in March and ends in June, when the weather there is unstable, with rain and sleet [*sic*], thunder and lightning. But in the dry season, which is usually constant throughout the rest of the year, there is a very strong surf at the shore. Three or four days before and after the full moon, just as several days before and after the new moon, and always during the first quarter of the waning moon, the tide is noticeably greater than otherwise. The daily tide can rise or fall usually by 3 feet, but during and immediately after the full moon it rises to 6 feet.

In Accra there are no more winds during the entire year than just 2 kinds, namely, the southwesterly from 7 o'clock in the morning to 9 or 10 in the evening, when it is replaced by the northeasterly from land, and lasts the rest of the time. And these land and sea winds alternate at all times.

//197// It is the case along the entire Coast that these winds alternate, as described above, but on the contrary, below Puni, which lies about 6 miles below Accra, there is along that entire coast no noticeable land-wind, but year in and year out a constant southwesterly, or sea-wind. However, it does happen during *travader*, which usually come from land although some do come from the sea, that it can last for 1, 2, 3, or even 4 hours, and there can be a great change in the usual winds.

Storms and severe weather are not experienced, to speak of, along the entire Coast, all the way from far above Capo Verde and far down to the Bight of Benin and Angola, and even farther. But when you are outside the breakers you could, with a small boat, sail over to America, as long as you could carry your necessary provisions of food and drink; since everything that lies below 47 degrees, between the two Tropics, can reasonably be called the peaceful sea, since the sea is very gentle the entire way. And sailors have so little bother and work, or discomfort, in those waters, that the skipper, nearly //**198**// every evening, makes them dance and jump around so that, because of all the inactivity in their lives, they would not become absolutely destroyed by scurvy. And although a good officer does have his daily duties to perform for the crew on board, yet there is no energetic exercise that could prevent scurvy.[90]

Otherwise, in December or January there occurs on the Coast, annually, a strong easterly wind that is called *armetanen*.[91] In the year 1710 it began on 19 Dec. and lasted until 30 December. This same wind carries with it an unhealthy fog and poisonous, dense, air. That wind is so dry and dessicating that the leather in your shoes cracks as you stand in them; binding loosens from the spines of books and actually shrinks; the skin on your lips, face and hands stings painfully as it cracks. It is, at times, painful enough for us Christians, but far more so for the poor, naked heathens. That wind lasts for 1 or 2, or even 3 weeks, and usually causes illness and great discomfort among the Christians, and one hardly fails to find attacks of fever during that time. //**199**//

---

90  Scurvy is caused by lack of vitamin C.

91  *Armetanen*/Harmattan is caused by the north-east trade winds carrying dust from the Sahara. It usually occurs in January and February.

# Chapter Twenty-four

Normally, during *travade* or rainy season, and at other times when there is rainfall, flying insects appear that are as large as fully-grown bees, but are actually a variety of flying ants. They have an intolerable stench, especially when you accidentally tread on one and kill it. Then you must leave the house because of the stench.

Besides the flying, stinking ants there is a variety that stays underground. They have a cave out of which they creep, usually when it is going to rain, or has begun to rain slightly, in order to gather their food. It is that variety which is much preferred by the pangolin, which I have described earlier.

Another, and larger variety of ants are found in great numbers. They gather in the same kind of ant-hills that we have in our country, but when the earth is still wet after a rainfall they mould the red clay or earth and build up their homes or hills, year after year, which, in many places in Accra, grow up in a pointed round shape like a pyramid. The ground area they cover is more that 4 *alen* in circumference, and they are, in some places, a good 6 or 7 *alen* high. //**200**//

In such anthills one finds an extremely good incense, at times lumps as large as a hen's egg, but the naked Negroes will not willingly come into contact with these red ants. They do not even set price by such incense. But if you wish to collect this – which is well worth the trouble – you must blast the anthill with gunpowder, because it cannot, without extreme effort, be broken down, since the intense [heat of] the sun has hardened the clay; and they cannot not be knocked over since they are very solid. Our black Boys could always go out into the fields a short distance from the fortress, and fetch a few small sticks of incense for us when we need it, but the best kind is found in the ground.

Further, in the wet season we are extremely bothered by mosquitoes in the rooms that are down on the ground floor, so that they drive the Christians from their houses and beds up to the open skies, [where] they lie at night on the batteries. They dare sleep in their own houses and beds scarcely once a week. And because of this nightly sleeping place and the dew which the people then breathe in and which settles in their chests, they experience not a little weakness in their bodies. Thus, it is with reason that Dapper calls these mosquitoes //**201**// a great plague. But the English, so that they will not experience the disgrace of mosquitoes having stung them to death, always, when they are on such journeys, wear trousers that reach down over their shoes.

These mosquitoes are much larger and more harmful at Qvita and Popo. Their sting is unbearable, and, after such a sting, if one scratches or tears it open – since it itches terribly – it swells up and often causes, among the Christians, serious and long-lasting sores on their legs, some of which remain quite incurable.

During the *travade* time there is still another difficulty, in that there are swarms of wild bees that visit the fortress and the houses, causing great discomfort. A couple of years ago they were guests in such great numbers in the pigeon-holes in the walls at Christiansborg that they absolutely drove the grown pigeons away, and killed the small ones, thus causing great damage, since the Christians everywhere on the Coast have a great preference for pigeons. Finally, they managed with great effort, and smoke, to drive these bees out of the fortress.

The people have shown great industry in taming and cultivating swarms of wild bees //**202**// for their own advantage, since [the bees] remain wild and unpredictable, like the people and the inhabitants. And no matter how well and prudently one treats these bees, [they do not] stay more than 8 days in one place, since the woods and the fields are far too full of food and well-scented herbs, flowers and trees.

Among all the dangerous animals found on the Coast the bush dog is nearly the most destructive. It is, therefore, that much more remarkable that that same [animal], as I noticed on 14 March 1710, is a special *fitis* for the Akras, but that is only when [the animals] are dead; since whenever they find a dead bush dog, everyone who passes his remains takes a branch of a bush or tree and throws it on [the body], as a sign of respect.[92] They hunt, and shoot, the living bush dog, hounding it to its death, but when it is dead, they do not dare touch the body, because then it is a god or sacred thing for them.

---

92 Rask is, perhaps, writing of the hyena.

# Chapter Twenty-five

Among the illnesses of the Akras I do not know if I can reckon pox [syphilis], or the so-called *fransoser*, since they do not consider it //**203**// to be a special illness at all. One even sees children apparently full of it. The reason for this is that children, when they are scarcely 11 or 12 years old, have intercourse with each other, like animals. Yet they do, by nature, have a particular revulsion towards incest.

Marriages among the Akras, and the Negroes in general, are not treated or carried out with any particular propriety, nor do they respect it very highly, since if a Negro, during a time of war, is so poverty-striken that he cannot get back by ransom his women who have been carried off by the enemy, he does no more than come to an agreement for one and one-half pesos, that is 6 rigsdaler, since that is what it costs him when he first takes her.

Everywhere they are very much afraid of foreign sailors, and in particular the French and pirates, because often, when Negroes have come on board they steal them away with them, and let the canoes float away. Therefore [the Negroes] are very careful and cautious before going aboard a foreign ship. Before any Negro on the entire Coast was willing //**204**// to come aboard our ship we on board had to fill a dipper of water, take some [water] with one hand, and let it run into our eyes and onto our faces several times. They never tie up their canoes to any ship that they do not know, but one of them stays in the canoe and paddles around so he can stay near the ship and receive his countrymen when they are ready to leave. But, should the Negroes who are on board notice the least sign of unfriendliness or any threatening movement, or, during their stay on deck, should there be sent shots from the ship to salute any other ship arriving or to greet a fortress, then, whether they are standing on deck, on the chain, on the quarter deck, in the forecastle head, or in a cabin, they fly out headlong and jump into the sea, and they can all swim like fish.

This is true of men all along the seashore of Guinea, that they all swim very competently, but I have never heard it told, nor seen, this among any women. Yet the women can wash themselves in the sea morning and evening, in a sheltered spot, although they usually carry water up to their homes, both for their own use and for that of their men and children. There the men and the other sex have their own places where they sit //205// and wash themselves. The women scarcely wade into the water over their knees. Even the girls do not go into company with the boys from the ages of 10 to 12, so that they could learn to swim, but as soon as they reach those ages they are kept daily at work, grinding millie and helping their mothers to bake, to brew beer and do other chores that must be done daily.

Indeed, I saw, daily, during our journey out here – when we had come to the Grain Coast and were still at the Tooth Coast [sic] – that when the Negroes had come aboard, if we wanted to throw old tobacco pipes, or some large glass beads, or old clothing into the water, although it was 20 fathoms deep, they could with great agility, dive under the water and fetch it up. But it must be noted that whatever we threw overboard never fell deeper than 4 fathoms before they had seized it. Our chief drummer, Christian Whit, could also do the same as any other Negro, but he told me that if he could not seize it before it went deeper than 4 fathoms, neither he nor anyone else could see it. He said that just as it is impossible //206// for a person on a ship to stand and see the seabed because of dark mud flats at a depth of 10 fathoms, it is nearly as impossible for a person, when he stands on the bottom, to see the sun and daylight over the water; but if it is a white sand bottom, he said, then one can see daylight just as through very thin glass.

The Negroes never carry any heavy burden on their backs or shoulders, but always on their heads. Among the Akras and the Akwamus there are many who could manage to use a swift horse . But for walking quickly with a large load no one can surpass the Negroes from Fida, who are small in stature as compared to the others. Therefore the Dutch and English fortresses everywhere are well supplied with company slaves from among those people. A Fidaish bearer, when he earns a day's bearer salary, which is 3 dambas or 12 shillings, carries a load of 100 pounds for 2 miles, and can go that distance so quickly, always humming or singing slowly to himself, that an Akra who is free and without any load can scarcely keep up with him. When there are 3 Fidas who //207// are carrying a hammock, although only 2 carry at the same time, they run with it at 10 miles in 10 hours, no matter how hot it is.

When a *kabuseer* or any other free Negro dies in Akra, the oldest son inherits the father's slaves and everything that he leaves behind, on the condition that he support his siblings until they can help themselves. But in Aqvambu there is a totally different system of inheritance: that one brother inherits from another, and takes over all his dead brother's wives as his own. [93]

The king at Fida takes over all his father's wives when the father has died, so that he has more than 500 wives, and he treats them all equally, except for his own mother, so absolutely animal-like are those heathens in their way of life.

The Fida Negroes let neither their hair nor eyebrows grow, but clip and shave themselves quite bald, so that although no Negro's hair grows long naturally, yet those at Fida are most free of all their hair, and quite bald.

When their king wishes to honour //208// a Fida by giving him some advantage, such as being in charge of others, even though the honour is always worn at an unworthy place, that *kabuseer*, then wears a cow- or tiger hide always hanging over his back, as his sign of rank, by which he can be distinguished from the others. Such a sign of rank must be seen to indicate no more than that he has been that much more bestial than the others.

---

93 The 'Akras' are Ga, a patrilineal people; the Aquamboes (Akwamu) are Akan, a matrilineal people.

# Chapter Twenty-six

The king of Fida must be seen, in his power, to be more like a prisoner than a free man, since the king of Aqvambu travels wherever he wants to, and is often on campaigns and at war during an entire year or more, but the king of Fida may not travel outside of his houses or residences. They claim that their *fitis* does not want it [otherwise] and there is no question of any other motivating reason, neither if it is to his advantage, or dangerous in general for all of his people.

If the question arises as to who their *fitis* is, it is as mentioned earlier, that it is a snake, which they worship like something holy and sacred. There are such indescribable numbers of snakes, and such tame ones that they are in company with them daily in their huts. //**209**// They lie with them in their beds at night, and this without their having the feeling that they are harmed by the snakes, as long as they take care not to anger them in the slightest manner. They also have a *fitis* house, full of snakes, standing out in the field, and if any Christian should be unlucky enough, either drunk or sober, to kill a snake, he would scarcely get away with his life if the Negroes should see it. Blessed Augustinus and others have written about such snake worshippers, which must seem almost unbelievable to us, if we had not found it absolutely true.

A number of Negroes among the Akras, when they have become ill, throw various things out into the paths, as gifts and presents for the devil, so that he will let them live yet a little longer, before he takes them. This is because they believe that the devil rules over illness and death, and that after death they come to the devil, but they do not fear this much, rather they wish for it, when things do not go their way.

I have been told by many of a Negro from Ursou, the *negeri* //**210**//

that lies under Christiansborg – called Hans Lyke after a [Danish] chief who had formerly been at Christiansborg – that he often wished he was dead, so he could go to the devil, since the devil, he said, *bringarer* [celebrates], or refreshes himself daily with brandy, palm wine and other good drinks; he has many women; he owns great cannons and a great deal of gunpowder with which to entertain himself. [This man] said he greatly wished to be in that company, and was sure he could deport himself as well as any [other] young devil. The Aqvambus beheaded that same Negro in a battle during the spring of 1709, just before I arrived in this country.

Another Negro, from that same Ursou, called Pajennen – who had participated in the dismantling of the Swedish trading house that had been here before, and had, along with other master masons, laid the first foundation of Christiansborg – believed, due to wondering about the quantity and variety of goods that were brought from Europe, that it was the devil who was the artistic master who made them and, then, gathered them at a certain place where the Europeans weighed //**211**// as much gold for him as they wished to give him as payment for the those goods. They laid the gold there, the devil was satisfied, took the gold, and the Whites, or Europeans, took the goods. All this amounts to the same idea, that, as they believe, everything that is more artistic than what they can manage to produce is a product of the devil's art. This has been told to me: that a man by the name of Halvor, here in Norway, who was very dextrous in producing certain artistic works was commonly called 'Halvor the Devil', and that that name, as well as his natural talent, has even been passed on to his children. So little is God honoured, who alone gives wisdom and reason and even creates the artist for that work – *Exod*: 31.3.4.

To touch somewhat on the Akras' mourning custom: when a man, or even just a child, dies at Akra, the women [*sic*], or the mother, put off all their finery of gold, aggreys, and beads together with whatever else they have; she shaves all her hair off, apart from a small tuft on the top of her head, throws an old *pankis* over her shoulders, and this is the mourning costume of the Akras. //**212**//

When anyone, young or old, among the Akras is to be buried, he or she must be interred in the best they own, and if the deceased owns gold, he or she takes it with him; since there is a proverb among them, that is, a law, that no one should be outfitted or decorated better than he would be for his funeral. Yet, nothing is worse than to dress the deceased ornately who need only to be covered before the eyes of the living, and await the corruption when they are laid in the earth, since they shall go naked from here. *Præd /Ecclesiastes*: 5.14.

If it is an Akraish child, or an inherited slave, or any unattached and free Negro who dies, they are usually buried at a special place behind the *negeri*. It is to this place that the closest friends of the deceased carry, weekly, some millie porridge, *ahaj* or beer, or brandy to the grave, and offer it in old pots or broken glass, which are left there for the *fitis*. If the deceased has some close friends who are wealthy, they usually build a roof over the grave, or put 4 small supports, about 3 feet high, one at each corner of the grave. On these they place 2 small logs, one on each side, which frame is kept evenly //**213**// covered with palm or coconut leaves. But if it is a wealthy Akra *kabuseer* who has died – although there are precious few of them now because the Aqvambus pick them off regularly – he is interred in a room in his house. And I have been assured that his sword and shield are placed in the grave with him, his shield under him and his sword in his right hand. They are not laid in coffins, of which they know nothing, but are set up in a standing position, as noted earlier.

# Chapter Twenty-seven

No *negeri* or village is so small but it has its recreational or playing and performing area, which is seldom seen to be empty, since they are very much given to games and gambling. This area is large or small, according to the condition of the *negeri*. The same place is used weekly as a market, where all manner of things are for sale, from both land and sea, for eating and drinking.

This same place is also used for formal occasions. For example, when a young Negro, especially among the Qvitas, takes his first wife – but not later, even if he takes 20 after that – they have the following custom. The wedding couple sit on 2 stools //**214**// next to each other in the marketplace, very quietly, for about 2 hours. Meanwhile, a Negro, who is their *fitissiero*, or priest, sits there and blows on a small pipe, but this is not a proper song, since they know absolutely nothing of such things. Accompanied by this wild piping and poor music, the Negroes who have been invited walk forward and present the bridal gifts to the bridal pair, *bussies*, millie, *pankis* (yet very small pankis in comparison to what the Akras wear, since the Qvitas, as the most immodest people I have ever seen or heard of on the entire Coast, go around mostly quite naked) and other such things for the wedding gifts. To take care of the gifts the lovely bridal pair have placed next to them sacks or tube containers. When the gift-giving comes to an end, they celebrate and enjoy themselves at the wedding, and this is under the open sky with a little to eat, but a superfluity of drink.

Their streets and roads in the *negerier* are only poorly kept clean so there is a right properly good smell; however, their own courtyards are usually neat and very clean. Along all the streets green trees have been planted, //**215**// 3 or 4 fathoms between each of them, which provide a comfortable shade and a lovely appearance, so that every *negeri* looks like a small green grove. They usually have long, overhanging rafters on their houses. All the way out to the street, as well as into the yards, they have clay benches along the walls [of the houses] where one can sit comfortably in the air out of doors, rather than inside their empty houses. At the end of the yard they have some small huts, some long, some round, which are purely for the women and slaves.

On the occasion of [my] reporting on the wedding customs among the Qvitas, I must also add that among the Akras and Aqvambus there are no extravagant customs when they marry, be it for the first time or the 10th time. The man gives the woman *pankis* and beads to [a value of] 3 *kabes*, that is one and one-half pesos, or 6 rigsdaler, as well as some brandy or palm wine. Then that business is finished, and for that price he can acquire as many women as he wishes.

Since I have now given a description of the Negroes' wedding celebration, I must add here //**216**// a short description of a common method of passing time, or buffoonery, that they indulge in. I have already reported that the Akras, as well as some other Negroes, have their special so-called propitious and unpropitious days, but in particular they also have a great feast, a *Grande Bon Di*, as they call it, a great propitious and good day, which usually comes in the month of August. Before Labade – which lies a *fjerding's* distance below Christiansborg – was destroyed in the Aqvambuish war in 1708 and 1709 this was called the *Labade Feast*.[94] However, it does not follow that Labade has ever been a kingdom, as Dapper reports incorrectly. But just as that celebration was formerly held annually in Labade, it is nowadays held in the Dutch *negeri* at Crevecoeur, a *fjerding's* distance above Christiansborg.

On that day, following ancient custom, there is a gathering of all the young men and women, boys and girls, and even if it means that they will starve for 8 days, they contribute their entire fortune for palmwine, brandy, *ahaj*, or Negro beer, and *kankis*, or bread to be purchased for this holiday and drinking party, to eat //**217**// and drink on that day,

---

94  The feast is clearly Homowo, described below, //223-26//.

to the sound of drumming, the blowing of horns, beating on basins, along with other ridiculous instruments.

But before I continue to tell about this it is necessary to describe their drums, to give the reader some idea of their delightful and pleasing music. Their drums are made in two ways: their *fitis* drums, which are rarely used apart from high holidays, are made of a whole log of wood, hollowed out to twice the depth of a kettle drum, but not nearly as large in circumference. Under the bottom there is also a hollow, or opening, but not nearly as large as the one on top. This drum is covered with parchment and stands on 3 wooden feet. Then there are their daily drums, that are not as high or large, made in the same way, covered with hide, and set between the drummer's legs when he is sitting, or it is hung on him in front, not at the side as we do, when he marches and plays. Sometimes they use drumsticks, sometimes they strike with their flat hands. There is another way that they make their hand-drums, since they also have //**218**// small hand-drums, put together of 2 small calabashes with hide at both ends. On these they fasten 4 very taut strings that go from the one end to the other, and one string is drawn round the middle of the drum. When stood on end it looks almost like a 6-hour glass. These drums are used by the women when dancing and rejoicing, being held under the left arm, and they strike them with 2 small drumsticks. As anyone can imagine, as is actually the case, neither is there any tone in such a drum, nor is it struck properly. But it quickly makes them dance, since dancing and jumping around are the greatest pleasure for both sexes, so that if anyone simply strikes an empty barrel with a couple of sticks, all present, with incredible energy, will hop and dance and jump, so that one can only wonder at it. Just as Dapper writes of the royal drums in Zenega, that they are held in high esteem, so are those among the Aqvambues. And the greatest ornaments that the Aqvambues' king has on his drum are the skulls of the foremost *kabuseers* //**219**// who have fallen in battle, which he hangs around his drum.[95]

Thus their drums. About their horn-blowing there has already been

---

95 For descriptions of drums and their use, see J.H. Nketia *Our Drums and Drummers*, 1968.

given a sincere opinion, and with the sound produced on such poor instruments they make their festivities right enjoyable: dancing and jumping, and now and then, in the midst of the dancing, they run towards each other, particularly the women, giving forth a horrible shrieking in one another's faces.

Besides the fact that their dances are laughable they are performed in a clowning way. When the men dance, since they do not join the women's groups, they have either a gun or a sword in one hand, and a shield in the other, with which they perform remarkable movements, and, in unbelievable ways, they can twist, turn and bend their limbs, and at times they perform such leaps that one fears for their necks. But they are unbelievably nimble and agile.

The women, on the other hand, dance alone: sometimes in a ring, and then one of them stands in the middle and answers the ones who are dancing around her. Sometimes //**220**// they dance in the English manner, two by two facing each other, but their legs do not move very quickly under them, since I believe I have never seen worse heel-draggers than the black women. It is like a fashion among them, but with their heads, arms and bodies they perform many comical movements. It should be noted, too, that the Negroes of both sexes dance and sing at the same time, not that they have any proper, rhyming verses or proper songs, as regards words and melodies, but they sing out whatever comes to mind; thus anyone can imagine what a poor combination of sounds is heard. If a Negro speaks to someone else, be it Christian or heathen, honourable or dishonourable, it must always be sung out. In this way they make known their sorrow and distress with a mournful song.

The word *girregy*, which Dapper calls the Negroes' *fitisse-laper* at Capo Verde, is always heard among the Negroes on the Gold Coast, humming when they dance, so that one must conclude that all this right foolish capering is supposed to honour the idol, since that [type of] //**221**// corrupted human reason can invent an unreasonable worship, when, in contrast, what God in his Word has decreed is everywhere holy and proper.

Their way of enjoying themselves on the Gold Coast, as well as with their instruments, have, indeed, been well described by Dapper. However, I have noticed two more things in Akra which I must add to those. First, when the fishermen celebrate they seldom dance, since they are of the opinion that dancing belongs to the people on land, but they sing that much louder and more powerfully. They have a round calabash, as large as a good-sized head of cabbage, that they hold in one hand and strike it on one end with the other hand when they are standing, but when they are sitting they strike it against their knee. Since this calabash is round and tightly covered with *bussies* and small brass or iron rings, it produces a very loud sound and rattle. Further, there is this: 2 females take hold of a rope, or the runner of a particular, otherwise useless, plant that grows there, a variety of plant that sends up from the root 2 or 3 runners which run everywhere along //**222**// the ground [for a distance of] more than 24 feet, and are as thick as a 3-inch rope. The women take a runner of a length of 3 fathoms, and both of them, together, swing it around as fast as they can; another one of them stands under the rope and can jump as expertly and quickly over it when, in swinging, it touches the earth, and the rope hardly once in 100 times hits her feet. Sometimes we see 2 jumping together over a rope, and they can turn around, jumping either on both legs or first on one foot and then on the other. And the one who holds out longest is praised, but the others ridicule the one who is too heavy and lets the rope hit her feet. This is a useful activity for them, but the Europeans cannot imitate them because they lack the stamina.

Before such capers begin, their *fitissiero*, usually the most complete rogue among them – who can conceive mostly lies and fraud with which to deceive these incredulous fools – makes a speech to them, and, as I have since investigated, //**223**// comforts them [by telling them] that although they are now subjugated by the Aqvambues, they shall, in time, become a mighty people, and have their own king again, as they had in former times. But he has no idea of how to urge them to lead chaste lives, much less to preach eternal trust or infallible hope for life in the hereafter.

On this, their high holiday, they are most ornately adorned. No matter how little they have, each one must wear a new piece of cloth, either wool or linen on that day, and their heads must be shaved in all manner of figures; and if they have any gold or aggreys those must also be worn on that day. One does frequently see Negroes of both sexes decorated in a ridiculous fashion, but especially on this great feast day they are well-smeared with palm oil or tallow mixed with finely ground coal, and then they set up their hair. Some of them, both men and women, also, instead of coal, use red earth that they grind up and mix with the oil in order to set up their hair. Some of both sexes make a thin dough of ground malaget, and this is //224// smeared, either over their entire bodies, or in close stripes, over their necks and under the shoulder blades, and down over their breasts. With this same mixture and in the same manner, they make stripes on their hands and feet; on their hands from the fingertips almost up to the elbows, so it looks like they have gloves on. And on their legs, from the toes up to the middle of the calf, not unlike old-fashioned Roman boots. And on their faces, which, however, is done largely by the other sex [i.e. women], they make stripes with the red earth, and small white chalk spots between the stripes, except in the middle of each cheek, where they set a white chalk mark as large as an 8-shilling piece, and this is their formal dress.

On the day before their great Feast of Fools they send one another gifts, that are usually stalks of millie, sugar cane, rolls or small round millie bread, *kabuseer kankis* or *master porridge*, that are made of finely ground millie, kneaded and cooked in water, then soaked in palm oil. Indeed, if they have nothing else, they send to their friend round sticks of firewood from which either the bark has been entirely removed, or on which a number of //225// irregular stripes, signs and crosses have been carved: so that he can build a fire with it, and warm himself. [96]

It should be noted here that that particular holiday is the Akras' New Year's Day, from which their new year begins, so those aforementioned gifts compare with our New Year's gifts. From this we see that although this folk – black and dark both externally and internally, as well as in

---

96 Homowo is desribed in many sources. See W.F.Daniell 'On the Ethnography of Akk-rah...'(1856) 29-32; A.B. Quartey-Papafio 'The Ga Homowo Festival'(1920) 126-34; M.J. Field *Religion and Medicine of the Ga People* (1937) 88-9; Asare Opoku (1970) 52-6.

their skin and hair – do not know what they are doing, or why they begin the year at that time; they can only cite ancient custom. Yet they closely follow the oldest and most natural reckoning of time: that the beginning of the year – in recognition of the natural course of the creation of the world – occurs in the natural condition when all products and fruits for the nourishment of animals are ripe. For this reason the month of *Thisri*, that corresponds partly to August and partly to September, was the first month for the Hebrews; despite their being ordered to keep the month of *Nisan*, being the exodus from Egypt, as the first month of their ecclesiastical year and in respect of holidays. Yet, in respect of trade and //226// purchase, rental and payment of taxes, the cultivation of the earth and its preparation, as well as the accounting of the [past] year, *Thisri* remained the first month, both in the time of Adam and the patriarchs, indeed from the calculation of the age of the earth . Just as the ancient Egyptians claimed that the world was created when the sun was in the end of the constellation *Libra*.

Just as in that [custom] regarding the beginning of the year, so do we, in other matters, find among the Negroes traces of the most ancient customs. For example: wherever a Negro is born, they usually carry him back there when he is dead, if it is at all possible. He is buried there, even if he, or she, died 10 miles away from the birthplace, almost in the same way, as the Scriptures tell us about the most ancient forefathers and their concern that they rest among their own people. And now I shall conclude this year's recorded matters, which I have, in a good state of health, recorded from time to time in this country during 1710.

# Chapter Twenty-eight

The year 1711, as well as the following year, was a miserably gloomy time, with almost continuous bodily illness and weakness. For this reason, as is usual //**227**// when the body is weak, the mind is unfit to notice and observe. Therefore there is nothing of interest recorded for that time, although what occurred daily, and was recorded in my weakened condition, now follows.

New Year's Day, 1 January [**1711**], thanks to a French sailor who had been in Porto Bello in March **1710**, we were given only bad news about both Guineamen, *Christ. Qvinto* and *Frid. Qvarto.* [He reported that] they lay there in poor condition, since 30 men of our people had gone to Martinica with a French ship; and both captains, with the rest of the crews, stayed with the ships, but without any hope of sailing the ships away from there.

In the same month, on the 13th, a Dutch interloper came into the fortress [*i.e.* the road], bringing us the somewhat strange news that the Negroes at Capo Tres Puntas had very strangely rushed away with the Brandeborger general, Mr. Lange – of whom information has been recorded above, on 9 March **1709**.[97]

On the 17th of the same month we received the news that the English governor-general at //**228**// Capo Corso had just died.

A few days later, on 27 Jan., Mr. Samson Walters, a merchant at the English fortress at Akra [James Fort], died. [He was] a particularly God-fearing and just man, my close friend, who was determined to learn the Danish language and had, therefore, asked to borrow a Danish book. However, since I did not have anything to help him other than

---

97  Actually, he had given this information on 24 March 1709 //**40**//

*Blessed D. Casp. Brokmands Postill* [a collection of sermons], I lent him that. He read through it with great industry and often said that he, in his heart, accepted and believed everything contained in it, and wished to live and die in that faith.

The next day, the 28th, we received the disturbing news that one of our soldiers at Christiansborg, by the name of Andreas Mikelsøn, had come from Qvita and reported that, on the 16th of that month, such a great number of large grasshoppers had landed there on the fields; and like the thickest swarm of bees, they had covered the earth completely for a good mile,. [These] were the same vermin that had earlier, on 25 Jan., been carried by the wind over to Aqvambu, which lies about 25 miles west of Qvita. //**229**// They had done great damage there in the millie fields, which were at their best just then, but, by shooting and a fire that was lit around the fields, they had been driven away, and took flight eastward.

In the morning of the 29th those same grasshoppers came, with the land wind, over Nungo and Tesse, about 2 miles east of Christiansborg; and on the same day, in the evening, they came over Labade, about a half-mile east of us. Thus, those places – Labade, Tesse and Nungo or Ningo – suffered considerable damage, especially since they had been weakened during the last Aqvambuish war. But they have never at any time been kingdoms, as Dapper presents them. All three *negerier* lie within an area of 2 small miles, and all 3 have formerly belonged to, and still belong to, the Akra kingdom. When they were at their most prosperous, which is not more than 30 years ago, Labade was the largest village among them, but could not have consisted of more than 500 men.

Finally, much too early on the morning of the 30th, those same uninvited guests arrived at Ursou and Christiansborg in indescribable numbers. //**230**// Others, along with me, were of the opinion that they had been born and grown up at Rio Volta, or the desert above that, because they came first from there, as far as we could discern. They were the same size as the largest green grasshoppers found in Denmark, but these were completely brown. I examined them closely, and asked everywhere if any Negroes ate them, but had the impression that the Guinean Negroes rather consider such a grasshopper swarm to be a *fitis*, or something sacred. Job. Ludolf's theory about such grasshoppers occurs to me, since he claims that the meat that Israel's people received in the desert: *Num: II.*31, 32 was not quail, but these grasshoppers, since quail er fatty birds and could not be measured in sacks, as Moses tells it. Furthermore, the Arabs either cook the grasshoppers, and eat them like shrimp – since in cooking they become red, too – or they kill them and hang them up by a horse hair in the sun for a day. Then they tie them together and eat them thus, wind-dried. Moreover, although we do not measure oxen and sheep in barrels, still we //**231**// customarily count them in so and so many barrels of beef or sheep meat. However, that swarm of grasshoppers did not stay with us long, since the Negroes chased them with fire and by shooting at them. They took flight again to the north-to-west, over Aqvambu, where there was more food for them than at Akra.

Our Deputy Assistant, Mr. Niels Hansøn, came from Breku on 5 March, and reported that, on the day before, he had heard about 20 cannon shots fired off slowly a few miles above. He did not know what it signified, but on the evening of the same day, there anchored at Christiansborg's road a Dutch interloper – the Captain's name was Thomas Planke – who reported that it was from his ship the shots had been fired for the Brandenborger general, Mr. Lange, who had come aboard him from Del Mina a few days earlier, in order to travel home to the fatherland with him, but had died on board on the same day that the shots were heard.

In the same month, on the 19th, came tidings from Del Mina that the Dutch inspector-general, Mr. Schonheid, who was mentioned on 14 July 1709, had gone //**232**// to his death a few days earlier; and that my most honoured friend, Mr. Hieronymus Haring, had, as the next in line, filled his post.[98]

In the meantime weakness overwhelmed me, so that it was only with great effort and difficulty that I could perform my duties; and since we heard time and time again of the death of so many Europeans, I often thought seriously about it. The best of all was that in those

---

98 He was mentioned on 19 July 1709.

conditions, God, in his loyalty, saved our people by giving them good health at all times.

Thereafter, on 28 June, one of our soldiers, by the name of Heinse Olsøn, went out into the fields with a dog in order to catch a hare. Normally one does not shoot such small game, but in the *travade-time*, when the grass is at its tallest, a good dog can track a hare or an antelope. As he had come a short way from the fortress, the dog began to charge furiously at a bush. The soldier, thinking that it must be a tiger, a bush-dog, or some other such animal, came running, well prepared, and saw that it was a snake, about 3 fathoms long, according to his report, and as thick as the upper part of a man's thigh. It was hissing and //**233**// threatening the dog, but at the arrival of the man the dog became more daring, and proceeded to attack the snake, which then raised up and dragged the dog under itself. The man, who was devoted to that dog, hit the snake with all his might with a large stick, which was his only weapon, and the dog was thus released. This so enraged the snake that it raised itself up, and with such great force struck out at the man that, had he not avoided the snake by throwing himself backwards to the ground, he would have been drawn under the snake, and hardly escaped alive from that poisonous great beast. Then, since the only protection he had with him was a large stick, he walked slowly home with his dog. But the dog had been sprayed with venom – which can serve to explain what happened later. [See] *Apocal*: 12.15, about what the snake sprayed out [*sic*] – and had received some venomous bites from the snake. It became swollen, and died in great pain during the night. This was undoubtedly because, as dogs always do, it had been licking the sores.

# Chapter Twenty-nine

Because on 24 August a Negro named Tete – who was living in the *negerie* Ursou close under Christiansborg – is to be made a *kabuseer*, he has been 'making custom', as they call it. //234// This is done in the following manner. He, along with the other *kabuseers* from Labade, as well as some of his friends from the Dutch *negerie*, Akra, gathered late in the evening, and during the night between the 4th and 5th August, entertained themselves by singing, horn-blowing, drumming and shooting. They certainly were forced to use that time because the heat of the day is so intense that it makes all pleasure impossible for people, and all activity laborious and uncomfortable. Thus, one rarely sees them so merry during the day as towards evening and during the entire night, when it is cool. And a *kabuseer* has no little respect, especially the *kabuseer* who is oldest in the Negro village; and I cannot adequately describe how great and loving is the respect each and every person displays, as if they were all his children, and whatever he orders or forbids is honoured with great obedience. A *kabuseer* of this rank usually has a special, open room in his courtyard – called his *palabercasa* [palaver house] – like a council room, where //235// they gather at night when they have anything to discuss, or anything special to work on together. In these gatherings that same *kabuseer* is, as he is usually called by the Portuguese, the *capitaneo* or chief. From this one can conclude what it means to become a *kabuseer*. And just such an honour was bestowed upon our Tete.

On the morning of 25 August the above-named candidate for the rank of *kabuseer*, accompanied by shooting, drumming, dancing and singing performed by his slaves, some 40 in number, came up under the fortress. He himself was decorated with gold and aggreys, on his head and around his neck, around his waist and legs, to a value of some 100 rigsdaler. He had a sword in his hand and a green wreath around his head. Directly behind him walked 2 young people, one carrying his gun and shield, which is an oblong, four-sided wooden frame covered with the hide of a tiger or buffalo. In the middle of it there is a handle of rope covered with leather where it can be held when he uses it in defence. The other [person] was carrying his gold in a small chest; but all around him //236// his own women and those of his friends were dancing. They were all carrying a green branch in one hand, and with the other hand they picked up earth and dust and threw it over the new *kabuseer*, all the while dancing and throwing earth on him, singing out his names – there are those who have 10 to 20 praise names – and by singing them they wish him all good fortune. It would seem to be a poor show of honour to cover him with dust and earth, but a Dutchman who had been in the country for many years, explained to me that, with the green branch that the women were carrying in one hand they wished that he should develop and flourish; and with the dust [it signified] that his offspring should be numerous. After that, when he had walked around, the flock followed him home again, and thus ended the celebration for that day.

After that, on 6, 7, and 8 August, he went, with his followers and in his fine attire, to the surrounding *negerier*, made visitations and received good wishes from the most prominent people at each place, who then gave him gifts to honour him. Some [gave] hens, some gold, some //237// aggreys, some beads, and more of that kind of thing. In the old days, as the Negroes themselves have told me, although they do not maintain it so strictly these days, no Akra could become a *kabuseer* before he had done at least 3 of 4 things, and if possible he should have done all 4. These were the things he should have done: 1. been in a battle, 2. felled an elephant, 3. a tiger, and 4. a buffalo. This is because the children of the *kabuseer* and of the others are always considered to be equals until they have distinguished themselves from the others by one or another praiseworthy deed. And it is known that both Aqvambues and Akras do indeed make much of a man who has felled one or several of the above-mentioned animals, and they are then called *bombofu*, that is, a good hunter or a good shot.

On the 17th day of the same month our new Chief, The Honourable Mr. Frans Boje, arrived, in good spirits, with health and life [intact]. The English ship that had bought him had sailed from London on 5 June and from Falmouth on 23rd, and had not had any trouble on the way.

At 6 o'clock in the morning of 25 October //**238**// our assistant, Poul Holst, died. He was born 18 July 1686, in Copenhagen, of prominent parents. His youth struggled against death, but he finally gave himself up to God's will.

At 4 o'clock in the afternoon of 13 November, our former Chief, Mr. Captain Erik Olsøn Lygaard, died, only 42 years and 3 months old. It is very strange that some Europeans, scarcely one out of 1000, reach a fairly advanced age; for the Creator, in his infinite wisdom, has ordered nature so that every land produces people so constituted that they can thrive and live there [in their own country].

It is the same in the case of herbs and trees: a number of European plants will grow in Guinea, while others do not, no matter how well one cares for them, as has been noted above. The same is seen in the case of animals: European chickens, ducks, geese, pigs and sheep thrive, but European dogs, on the other hand, can not tolerate it here. I have seen many examples of this, since Mr. Edvard Smit sent to his brother-in-law, Mr. Fran Boje, our Chief, over a period of time, more than 6 hunting dogs, but 3 weeks //**239**// after their arrival they began to be terribly mangy; then they got such violent diarrhea that they were weakened to death. But dogs that are brought from Brazil or the islands in America, can live there and remain strong. Yet, I have seen several of the small, short-haired, Spanish whippets who have been there on the Coast for more than a year.

# Chapter Thirty

Cats may have been originally brought there by the Portuguese, since there are absolutely none inland among the Aqvambues, unless they have bought them or received them as a sign of honour from the Akras. It is absolutely necessary to have them for the sake of the merchants' goods in the warehouses, and for peace in the the houses and rooms, since there are many, and large, rats, but I do not recall ever seeing a mouse. We have, most often, very little success with male cats because it is extremely difficult to coax them inside. I cannot actually give a reason for this. Yet I have noticed with a couple of female cats I had, that when they came indoors in the morning, they smelled very strongly of civet, so that they filled the room with that scent; //**240**// so I have concluded that they crept under the gate at night, and then jumped over the wall in the outwork and joined the civet, or *desmer*, cats who come in under the fortress from the fields every night, and have played with them. In which case the desert cats must have preferred to consort with the female rather than the male cats.[99]

These *desmer-cats* are actually the cats of the country, [and] when they become tame they get on better with other cats than with dogs, so they are undoubtedly of the cat species; despite their not having sharp claws like cats, nor do they have such soft fur. Instead, when they become angry or frightened, their hair stands on end and they hiss like a cat. Otherwise, in size, head and feet they resemble a fox, except for the fur along their backbone, which is short, straight and stiff, like that of a pig. [And like a fox] they are very sly in catching chickens. Their fur is grey with black spots and a black stripe along the back. If you get

---

99 *Civet tictis civetta.*

them when they are small you can scarcely determine which is male and which is female. But because there is a greater advantage in owning a male rather than //**241**// a female, you try not to purchase females, since they pollute the civet with their water, which always goes into the civet pouch that sits close under their tails, and that fluid makes the civet useless. But the male cats, whose civet secretion is always best, can be recognized because their fur is thicker, and their heads longer, than those of the female. Otherwise, when you get them as very small, you can raise them and have great pleasure with them, since they are clean, and much more entertaining in their play than [ordinary] kittens. But the very ugly habit these animals have is that, if they can manage it, they drop their unclean waste into the same container that holds their food, and from which they eat. They are quite willing to allow the civet to be taken from them, which it is necessary to do every 4th or 5th day. Otherwise they rub and scrape it off against whatever they can find. They must, more properly, be called civet rather than *desmer-cats*.[100]

In the year **1711**, in the month of May, I observed the Akras' idolatry regarding their *fitis*-harvest. When the fruit, or root yam, described above, becomes //**242**// fully grown, which is usually in May, the Akras, both young and old, male and female, make their offering to their *fitis* in the following way. Each one purchases a couple of shillings worth of the yam, cooks it in a pot until it is a thick porridge. They then set this porridge outside their doors, or in the corners of their *casas* or houses. This is rarely on the bare ground, but they cut small sticks about a finger-thick or less, and a quarter [*alen*] long. These are scraped until they are beautifully white, then bound 30 to 40 together, and buried halfway upright, with the ends in the ground at these places. Onto these they dole out the yam porridge. However, before this annual sacrifice is made, [that bundle of] sticks must have been sprinkled with the blood either of a pig, sheep, goat, chicken, or, if nothing else, of a dog. They deceive themselves into believing that their *fetis* eats this, and will then give them life and good fortune that year. Upon seeing this I could not but remember our Danish expression *'Det staar paa Pinder for dig'*,

---

100 *Desmer* is the Danish term for both civet and musk, so Rask seems to be suggesting that 'civet' is the more precise term in this case.

which, had there not been such great distance between Denmark and Guinea, would easily suggest //243// that the custom had its origin [in Denmark].[101]

That same month I was shown the egg of a crocodile, or kaiman, which was as large as that of a fully grown hen, but more oblong, and the shell was blue with black spots. The gall of the kaiman is, as I have been told, the most deadly poison, into which the Negroes dip their arrows. The wound caused by such an arrow is absolutely incurable, unless one can remove the entire limb immediately, or, at least, cut a very large piece out around the point of impact.

As I write about this poison, I cannot but recall a number of other poisonous animals, which are found in abundance there. *Hagadis* is a variety of reptile, which can run quickly both up and down the walls. It lives in cracks in the walls. It lives on ants, scorpions, millipedes and other such crawling animals. When they are in disagreement and fight with one another, they hit each other with their tails, in which lies their greatest strength. They lay eggs almost as large as sparrows' eggs.[102] //244/

Scorpions are found in no smaller numbers, and they can be found easily when it drizzles, when they come out of their homes in the earth or under stones or piles of stones. The can do no damage to you if they run over your body or limbs, but if you happen to touch them on the back, they immediately strike with the poisonous, pointed, claw that is on the end of the tail. It is rarely that you can find out when you have been stung, but as soon as you feel the appearance, be it ever so small, of a painful swelling on your limbs that were healthy just previously, it is the sting of the scorpion. Then those [living] in Guinea usually apply scorpion oil. The ordinary men there – who usually walk barefoot, since a pair of poor stockings and shoes cost as much as 3 rigsdaler – are very often stung by this poisonous vermin. Using thumb and index finger – which grip the Negro always uses – and grasping it on both sides of that claw, he can pick up, without injury, as many scorpions as he

---

101 The Danish phrase: literally, to 'stand on sticks for you' – idiomatically, to 'be at your beck and call.'

102 This is probably a gecko.

wishes. The largest scorpion I have seen was like a small crayfish, about 4 inches //245// long. I saw one at the home of the Dutch surgeon, Per Kundiger – who was born in Itsehoe – who had one hanging [in his room] as a curiosity, because of its size.

The millipede – so called because of the many feet it has – is found there in considerable numbers, and is held to be even more poisonous than the scorpions. They injure by biting, and their bite is extraordinarily poisonous. I have not seen any that were more than 5 inches long. In order to have remedies at hand against the poisonous bite of these vermin, you are always provided with either millipede oil, or you let them drown themselves in the bottle of that oil – in which the scorpions also drown, and the poison dies because of this oil. Thus, without a doubt, the Almighty Creator has so arranged nature that people would exert themselves to destroy such poisonous creatures, since in their death is found the cure of their injury.

# Chapter Thirty-one

In September that same year I became aware that some women, with laughter and joy, were throwing earth and sand over another woman, which I thought [was being done] //**246**// because she had committed a misdeed. But I found out that this was a formal affair, since, when a fisherwoman among the Akra finds herself pregnant with the first child, she must suffer the other women to throw dirt and dust and sand over her. They loosen all her hair locks, since her hair must also be soiled. Thereafter she runs as fast as she can to the beach, submerges herself several times, and washes herself thoroughly. The others, who have followed her to the beach, stand on land, meanwhile, singing, shouting and dancing. When she has washed herself – although she is no whiter than she was before – she goes home, where her closest friends shave her head and set her hair again [*sic*], decoratively, in their opinion. I compare this illogical show of honour with that where I observed women throwing dust over a *kabuseer* as a wish and signifying that his issue should be numerous.

However, when the wife of a *mercador* [merchant] among the Akras is pregnant for the first time, she goes around naked for the last 4 months, //**247**// bound around her waist with 6 or 7 layers of glass beads, and wears sometimes a sheepskin, but most often a deerskin, in order to cover her lower abdomen. From her wrist nearly to her elbow she wears, meanwhile, instead of beads and aggreys, straw and whisks of straw. When she has given birth to her first child she makes a cap of that above-mentioned animal skin for her husband. From the day an Akraish woman discovers that she is pregnant with her first child, the father does not shave his head or beard, but lets the hair grow freely.

No Akraish Negress, when she is carrying a child, drinks any kind of drink completely, but rather, she always spits, of her own will, a little of it onto her abdomen, saying that the child is having a drink. When such an Akraish woman is going to give birth for the first time, as far as it is possible she is taken to her own place of birth in order to deliver the baby, but later //248// at the birth of the second or third child this is no longer observed.

I have reported earlier that circumcision is practised among all the Akras, and can now just add the following, that among the Fidas they are so strict about circumcision that an uncircumcised man cannot be their king, regardless of how entitled he is.

The Negroes along the entire Guinea Coast know nothing of dividing the year into its months or 4 main seasons, yet they do observe the moon and know from that how to count their lucky and unlucky days, as well as the recently described Labade feast. In the same way, the man on the land knows when to plant this or that kind of plant or fruit; no less do the fishermen know when this or that kind of fish comes or goes.

The Negroes who live near the fortress and are in daily contact with the Christians, do not know how many hours we reckon for a day and night, yet they know from the sun when it is midday. But they themselves do not use hours or the divisions of the day, as can be seen among the Blacks inland who know nothing of such things. //249//

But if they know nothing of reckoning hours, they do know that much more about how to attend to the fancied ornamentation of their bodies; just as Iob. Ludolf writes about the Abyssiniens that, when they have smeared their entire bodies, and the hair on their heads has also been smeared and set up, in order that this ornamentation will not be disarrayed when they sleep, he says that they have a staff shaped like a hay fork, whose shaft they place into the ground and lay their neck and cheeks in the cleft so that their head lies with the hair hanging down, a little above the ground. Likewise, the Guinean Negroes everywhere, and of both sexes, use small wooden stools nearly one-half *alen* high, very carefully carved. The upper part of the stool is hollowed in the shape of the moon in its first quarter, and is 3 inches high at the highest.

Upon this they always lay their heads when they are resting, for the same reason as described above.

Wherever any *kabuseer,* and even the commoner, goes he has his *dreng* [Boy] with him, who carries 2 stools; one for his master to sit on, and the other, as already described, when he wants to lie down and sleep. Whenever a prominent *kabuseer* comes in a lively procession //250// he usually has a following of 20 to 40, even more, young men, some with guns and swords, others with lances and spears called *hasagajer.* One *dreng,* as noted above, with the stool; one with the tobacco pouch and pipes, which have very large heads and, stems at times 2, even 3 *alen* long. One has a bundle on his neck [comprising] his master's bed, made up of a tiger or buffalo skin, 3 or 4 small reed mats, and a couple of thin blankets.

If a *kabuseer* comes on an important errand he always has a *dreng* with him, called a *titi,* who, either in the place of meeting or in the house where the business is to be negotiated, claps his hands so that everyone will be quiet, while his master speaks and states his business. That particular *dreng* can be recognized thus: that he always has a broom, or fan, in his hand with which he makes a breeze to cool his master, and brush flies and mosquitoes away from him. That same *dreng* always has a black, or grey, long-haired monkey skin on his head. Recently a *kabuseer* had with him a group of young men, some of whom blew horns made //251// either of rams' horns or small elephant or sea cow tusks; some played drums, some struck a small iron or copper plate with a large, old nail.

On this occasion I must relate a remarkable custom, honoured everywhere among the Negroes. If anyone, be it a Whiteman or Black-man, sends his *dreng* somewhere, carrying his staff, no one dares to touch or harm him, since this signifies a safe pass and [symbol of] safe-conduct, of which they know nothing. But this custom closely resembles the runner's baton, which is used among us and is, in the same way, a sign of safe passage.

When anyone travels there on the Coast, either to trade or for other business, [at places] where he wishes to spend the night or stay for any length of time, he must report to the most prominent *kabuseer* at that place; since if he has anything outstanding with any Negro in that town, the *kabuseer* must make it clear that if he should demand anything there, or do anything that is unconventional, or seize anyone as a pawn – whether it is a free or unfree Negro who will be taken as a pawn – or if it be gold or aggreys, and the *kabuseer* there is not a party to it, //252// then everything that is done is of little or no value; and his demands are either officially opposed or outright denied. And if anything is taken from him while he is staying there, which can easily occur, since the Negroes are very clever at thievery, then the *kabuseer* should – if he had reported to him upon arrival, which should properly be done – make good [the loss], which does happen. Otherwise the loss is his, unless, even after a very long period, he can succeed in seizing someone or something on the account of the one who injured him; since then the friends of the seized person, or the owner of the goods, take it very seriously that payment must be made even to taking the life of the guilty one, according to an unbreakable rule among the Negroes – as mentioned on p. 193 – who will take his own life on the account of their enemy.

# Chapter Thirty-two

The most abominable proof of their heathenish wickedness – an unavoidable result of the brutish abuse and corruption of [the institution] of marriage – is the inhuman relationship between parents and children. A Negro //253// can freely, and with impunity, beat his child to death, or sell it, or drown it if it cannot recover from some old, persistent weakness, which very often occurs among this brutish folk, among whom one finds little wit, and absolutely no conscience. And love among these beasts cannot possibly be found to any greater degree than among animals. When a man can have 20, 30, 40, indeed 100, 200 and more wives which is not a rare occurrence – and of the many wives there are a number of children who know little of their mother, but far less of their father, since he plays little or no attention to them, how can one expect anything else, than what one sees here regularly: that parents strive to dupe the children, and children their parents; and given the chance, the son just as soon sells his father or mother, as does a father his child, except for the time when the children are young, then the father equally freely sells his son or daughter as one of our men sells his pig.

But if a Negro beats one of his wives to death, or sells her without good reason, //254// then, as long as she has some friends, they do not allow this to go unchallenged. If, however, she has no friends, no one asks about her any more than any one of us would ask when a man sells his sow, or shoots his dog to death. Yet, how holy, just and good is not God's Word? How can one not love, honour and respect that Light highly enough? And what praise, honour and gratitude are we not duty-bound to show that Eternal God!

When I was weak, in December 1711, our deputy-assistant, who had travelled to most of the places in Guinea and was especially knowledgeable about their way of life, told me, for the refreshment of my spirit, about a custom that is observed in Lampe, which lies about 30 miles east of Christiansborg, but inland. [He related] that after a Lampe Negress has given birth to her first child, when it is a couple of days old they decorate it with beads and aggreys, because they do not have gold there, nor do they care particularly about it. They place a green wreath, also decorated with aggreys and beads, on the child's head. Then the maternal grandmother, if she is still alive, or another woman from //255// among the closest friends of the mother, carries it around to each man in the *negeri*, who, according to his own wishes, gives the child a gift. This parade proceeds in this way: first there go 3 persons from the mother's side; then she who is carrying the baby; after her goes the father's mother, if she is alive – which is most often the case since they come together early and beget children – or a women from among the father's friends; and finally, last in line, 3 women from the father's side. What is collected in this way is like a christening gift to the firstborn.

This noticeable difference, everywhere among the Negroes, between the first-born and the others, indisputably – just as their circumcision and other things – comes from God's ordering of law to the Israelites and their forefathers: that the first-born, who is an important image of The Great One, and all the creatures' first-born: *Col*:1.15, was chief and master over all his subjects, and was, during the time of Moses, heir to all his father's goods: 1. *Book of Moses*: 24,36,25.5. And thereby is the solution //256// of the difficulty that some of the interpreters of the Scriptures have, that Jacob was so poorly equipped by his father Isak, with only a staff in his hand: 1 *Book of Moses*: 28.1 and 32.10. They give their imaginations free rein: that Isak, in his old age, must have become so weakened: that Isak could not give Jacob anything, since Esau, who still held claim to being the first-born, was the heir to all his goods. But after the time of Moses the first-born was heir to 2 parts. 5 *Book of Moses*: 21.17. Thus, when the youngest son in the parable is cited as saying, 'Father, give me that part of the estate which is mine by right', he was requesting the 3<sup>rd</sup> part, to which he was entitled, and the rest went to his eldest brother; to which the father says, 'Everything that is mine, is yours'. *Luc*: 15.12.31.

In the same way I have been told that when some Kræpæes – a people who live 25 miles below Christiansborg, to the east, but at the shore – follow their custom that when a man becomes engaged to another man's daughter when she is still an infant, it is most common among them //257// that he gives [the father] a bridal gift of 8 or 10 strings of glass beads, which the child, to honour him, must then wear at all times, and it is proof that she is a betrothed girl. Her parents must give him a *cabes bussies*, which is as much as a half peso or 2 rigsdaler. When the man thinks she is grown enough, he releases her from her parents with another *cabes bussies* or 2 rigsdaler. Then a day is decided upon as the wedding day, when the bridegroom sits outside his house with some of his relatives and closest friends. The bride arrives, led by her closest relatives and family members. As soon as she has arrived they greet each other with 3 handshakes, which is the method used for greeting common among the Negroes everywhere in Guinea, as mentioned before. Then he drinks to her from a calabash of *ahaj* or millie beer. But as soon as she has received the bowl in her hand, her fiancé strikes it out of her hand, and, in great haste and excitement, the fiancée backs into the house. Then all her friends go in to join her, and wish her good fortune; //258// and from then on she is not allowed to go out into any public gathering with others until it can be seen that she is pregnant. This must occur after 8 or 10 months, but if an entire year passes and there is no sign of fertility, [her husband] pays her no more attention.

But if he becomes engaged to a woman who is fully grown, they do not perform the first custom, but only the last one after the wedding day, as described above, and from then on she is constantly observed. If the woman does not become pregnant within the course of the year since she had come into the man's house, he pays no more attention to her, but, as unfit for childbirth, she is absolutely ignored, or is only used in the future as a slave.

# Chapter Thirty-three

In the *negeri* Temma, those who live there observe an annual idolatrous holiday, which our Deputy-Assistant, Mr. Niels Hansen – who had been present himself and seen it – described to me. Every year, in April, they make their *fitis*, which for them is a tiger. They sacrifice 1 ox and 2 sheep. Before they slaughter the ox, 12 of their men take hold of //**259**// first the ox and then the sheep, separately, and lift them up into the air 3 times. When they have skinned them they divide the hides among themselves, and they treat the internal organs so uncleanly that I am unwilling to describe it to my honourable readers. Yet, they cook them along with the meat, and when they have then been made edible, they eat all of it. The well-cleaned heads of the animals are placed on *fitis*-stakes, made of round logs or stakes, that are pounded 1, 2, or 3 together in a cluster into the earth, and covered with white and red chalk. It is the *fitis* that shall have this as his share, and perhaps it is true that this is enough for him, but one must admit that this is a strangely ingenious way of worshipping their god, to eat all the meat themselves and give the *fitis* the bones. I assure you that if they could eat [the bones] themselves, he would not enjoy even them. What is the most formal in this is that the heads of the animals are given the honour of being set on stakes, since the Negroes' *fitis* altar is made up of stakes or poles which stand vertically [in the ground].

But it is really remarkable, that, if any Christians are present, they are invited //**260**// very formally to [participate in] this sacrifice, although no Christian is either such a heathen or so foul that he would let himself be persuaded to be their guest. But no uncircumcised Negro may enjoy any of it. When the heads of the sacrificial animals have been set on the stakes, [the Negroes] dance, sing and jump around the the *fitis*-stakes standing in the marketplace for 8 days, and their *fitissiero*, or priest, plays the drums for them as merrily as he can. For his trouble he is given 1 *damba*, worth 4 shillings, from each Negro in that *negeri*. This sacrifice is made so that their *fitis*, which is a tiger, will give them dry weather and good luck in their salt-making that year. He [Hansen] also told me that when the millie is half-ripe they have an idolatrous holiday, making a large sacrifice in the same way, but he had not been present to see it himself. But may God be praised who has taught us to serve The Living God and worship Our Lord Jesus Christ's Father in spirit and truth! And I close here, in this my year of weakness **1711**, which I have since discovered was because of the destructive plague, also was a year of weakness for my fatherland. //**261**//

We began the year **1712**, by the grace of God, in a fairly desirable condition, to the honour of God's Most Holy Name, since both the officers and the garrison were in good health, and I, myself, was sufficiently well to be able, with the help of God, to carry out my duties without too much difficulty.

But, on 16 January it pleased God to take away the use of his mind of a member of the Company's military force – a man by the name of Niels Johansøn Kattenberg – to such a degree that he had to be put away and kept under lock and key; and he was still thus locked up in that wretched condition when I took my farewell with the fortress. And although, in the practice of my position, I both visited him at times and primarily as God's official servant, as well as in my daily services I prayed to God for him, yet I heard the comments of a number of injudicious persons who felt that I should have preached God's Word to him until he recovered. But just as one can preach to a deaf person until he can hear, so could one preach to a demented person until he regains his reason; since preaching of God's Word can achieve nothing //**262**// without a listening ear and an understanding heart.

In the beginning of February my weakness returned, and remained unchanged for 3 months. [During that time] the duties of my office were insuperably difficult for me, more so than I can describe. This was noticed by everyone, and I was given much sympathy for my frailty.

On 9 June a strong and active female slave at Christiansborg died of a poisonous bite in her thigh. She had been bitten 8 to 10 days earlier while she lay asleep in the prisoner – or slavehouse [baracoon]. As soon as this became known she was treated with all the remedies against poisoning in order to save her life, if possible, but it was clearly too late. The snakes in Fida are far more friendly – which can be seen on p. 209 – than they are here in Akra: where this, as well as many other examples, bear witness to the fact that it is only unreasonable gossip that many in my fatherland believe, that a snake never harms a sleeping person.

Finally I experienced the month of September [1712] as my last month at Christiansborg //263//, which, in fact, I expected would be my last month here on earth. But God wished it otherwise. On 10 September, at 4 o'clock in the morning, a member of our garrison, by the name of Peter von Wovern, died. He was a decent, indeed a right godfearing man, born of a good and well-known family. He had become ill at the same time as I had the year before, and from that time and until the day of his death, neither of us enjoyed [as much as] 2 months of good health, all told. Doing my duty, but in a weakened condition, I comforted him in his last hours, thinking that I would be the next one to follow him into eternity.

# Chapter Thirty-four

Since I recognized that my health would no longer tolerate staying there, on 16 September I delivered to the Commander, the Honourable Mr. Frans Boje, and to the Council at Christiansborg, my request that, considering the present circumstances, they accept my resignation. This was granted me on that same day, so I need feel no shame in that respect.

Thereupon, on 29 September, I officially took leave of my position, //**264**// and with all my heart commended my congregation, hitherto in my trust, to God and His Mercy, which are powerfully edifying. And I left there that same evening, in the Name of God.

On 30 September, very early in the morning, I arrived at Breku, which I left that same evening.

On 1 October, at 9 o'clock in the morning, I arrived, tired and exhausted, at Appam, but could not stay there, and travelled from there at the approach of evening.

On the 2nd of the same month, in the morning, arrived at Anemabu, and, luckily for me, I found there an English ship from Barbados, captained by my old friend Jacob Byrgesøn. I rested on his ship the entire day and the following night, which was wonderfully refreshing for me.

In the morning of the 3rd I left there, and towards midday continued towards Capo Corso, where I remained the following day.

On the 5th the English agent, the honourable Mr. Seth Grossner, lent me a hammock and 4 company slaves who carried me to St. George Del Mina. There I found my much respected friend and great benefactor, //**265**// the Dutch Governor-General, most honourable

Mr. Hieronymus Haring, in a desirable state of health. Since he was ready to travel up the Coast, he invited me to keep him company, which pleased me because the English warship, *Falmuth*, on which I had been promised I could travel home to England, lay there at Capo Tres Puntas, and I did not know if it would sail from there to America.

On 6 October Mr. Haring and I arrived at the Dutch fortress at Commendo, and towards evening at Skema, which also belongs to the Dutch. Everywhere I was treated with great respect, for Mr. Haring's sake, and by this travelling from one place to another, and Mr. Haring's solicitous care, I found my condition much improved over my long-standing weakness.[103]

On 9th of that same month we left Skema and arrived, on the same day, at the Dutch Fort Secunde. The most remarkable thing I found there were 2 metal cannons, one a twelve-pounder, on which there was inscribed, in clear letters: *Philippus 3. Rex Hispaniæ: 1603*. The other was also a Spanish cannon, //**266**// an 8-pounder, on which was engraved the Granadian coat-of-arms. Immediately below this Dutch [fort] lies the English Fort Secunde, which is a particularly fine and well-equipped little fort. General Haring and I ate very well there, as if it were in London.[104]

On the 12th we left together, with great shows of honour at our departure from Secunde.

And arrived the day after, the 13th, in the afternoon, at the Dutch fort Butru, where we had to stay, because of an annoying matter, until...[105]

The 14th, in the evening, when we could leave there; and on 15 October, we arrived at the Dutch fort Axim. There I found, to my good fortune, the English Sub-Agent, Sir Jacob Phips, who, because of our pleasant acquaintance earlier in Akra, received me very heartily and spoke eagerly on my behalf to Sir Riddel, Commander of the English warship *Falmuth*, who was then present. [Sir Riddel] promised me

---

103 The Dutch fortress was Vreedenburgh; the fort at Shama was originally built by the Portuguese but taken over and rebuilt by the Dutch in 1640 (van Dantzig *Forts and Castles of Ghana*, ix).

104 The Dutch fort at Secondi was Fort Orange; the English fort was built in 1682 but there are no traces now (*ibid.*)

105 The Dutch fort at Butri, originally a Swedish lodge, was Fort Batensteyn (*ibid*).

good conveyance on my journey homewards, by way of England. And in all this I cannot sufficiently wonder at God's paternal providence, which has evidently followed me //267//; and I am unable to express this sufficiently for all the others who fear God.

Since now, with God's good hand over me, I was clearly assured of the desired opportunity to go to England, I took my leave of the Dutch General, Mr. Hieron. Haring, and indebted as I was to him, I thanked him, whom God had provided as a medium for my aid; and the same evening betook myself on board along with the English Commander Riddel. But I cannot refrain from telling about the strange effect that separation from Mr. Haring had on me. As reported on 6 October, in his friendly company and the enjoyment I found in it, I was quite freed of my long illness. Thus I must, in all honesty, say that, in spite of the kindness and attention shown me by the English Commander, as well as by all those both of high [rank] and low on the English ship, yet, counting from the very moment that I left Mr. Haring, I found myself ill again. To such a remarkable degree can a free spirit and content mind affect //268// the health of the body. This is very well in agreement with God's wise, firm and true Word: *Præd:[Eccles.] 8.15.*

Directly, the day after I had come on board, on 16th, we weighed anchor on the ship *Falmuth*, and towards midday we anchored again under Capo Tres Puntas, where we remained for 4 days.

Equally, on the 17,18,19 and 20 the English Commander Riddel, the Dutch General Haring, the English Agent Phips and the Brandenborger General du Boys had important business to attend to at Great Frideriksberg, concerning what was told us earlier, on 13 January 1711 at Christiansborg.[106]

At 4 o'clock in the afternoon of 21 October we sailed away from there, but because of sudden calm we only made one mile, namely to the Brandenburger trade office Takelma, where we had to drop anchor.[107]

On the 22th, at the break of day, we weighed anchor again, and

---

106 See above //155//. But the year mentioned there is 1710.

107 Probable reference to the Brandenburger lodge *Louisa* at Takrama (van Dantzig 1980, ix).

towards midday we anchored under the English Fort Dikesko [Dix-cove], where we had to stay for 3 days in order to take on firewood and water.

On 25<sup>th</sup>, in the morning, when we were //**269**// fully provisioned, we left there with a slight wind.

On 26<sup>th</sup> October, at about midday, we reached Capo Corso, where, in order to obtain all the necessities for the voyage to Europe, we stayed for 7 days.

On 2 November, in the morning, we took our leave of Capo Corso, but as we were in the process of boarding, an English ship came from the sea, captained by Captain Hotson, who dropped anchor in the road. He called out to our Commander Mr. Walter Riddel, "10 percent Captain!", whereupon our Commander, along with Captain Hiumer of the English ship called *Mary Galley*, went aboard Hotson's ship.[108] There they found an irreparable leak. In respect of the Coast of Guinea, there is no possibility for repairing a fault like that, since the ship draws more than 6 feet; and Del Mina is the only place where help can be found. Since the crew dared not go on to seek help at St. Thomas [São Tomé], lying at the equator, it was their duty to help the man. Therefore with boats, sloops and dinghies, expanding great effort, they unloaded the ship in less than 3 days. //**270**//

On 5 November, when the ship's entire cargo had been saved, they had to let the hull drift into land.

Then, at daybreak on 7 November, we finally weighed anchor, in the name of Jesus, in order to go to Europe, and see again the land of our fathers.

During the time we were on the warship *Falmouth*, no one was ill, apart from one apprentice who died on 15<sup>th</sup>, and was buried according to the manner on board ship, quite without any ceremony.

---

108 *'Ten percent, Captain'* obviously means that he is offering 10% of the value of the cargo in return for help.

# Chapter Thirty-five

On the day after, the 16th, by taking our bearings from the sun, we found ourselves to be 15 miles north of the equator, and 1 hour later we had land in sight, which was the island of St. Thomas. This lies right on the equator, and is a large island, fully 10 miles both in length and breadth. It is said to be a very unhealthy country to live in, and is nearly always covered by fog, just as it appeared to us then.

On 17 November we sailed out, staying along the northern side of that island, which we saw was just as covered by mountains as any land in the north, but otherwise very fertile. The Portuguese //**271**// have a small trading place there which, however, had been much plundered in war. The inhabitants there have some ships that sail to Africa and America for slave trading, but that is of little consequence.

And here, in this repect and with the favourably disposed reader's permission, I must report something concerning the slave trade, which I noticed with great emotion. When the merchant who is carrying on this abhorrent trade comes to the fort or trading station with slaves to sell, all the slaves have their hands tied behind their backs, but they are without irons or bolts on their feet. Around the waist of the first slave there has been bound a rope of raffia, or of some other material, and the rope is long enough to be drawn under the right arm of the one behind – for as many as there are. In this way the owner and his people drive these poor people altogether in one line, like beasts. In truth, my eyes often ran with tears at this sight, and I was reminded of what is written in *Apostles: 2 Tim: 2.26.*

The slaves must be carefully examined by the doctors and surgeons at the fortresses, to see if there are any faults, //**272**// and be [the faults] ever so slight, internally or externally, the slave is immediately discarded, or the price is lowered. For this reason one must hide knives, and everything that is sharp, from the slaves, since it has often happened that they cut off either their fingers, or toes or ears, to avoid being sold.

If a Negro, free or unfree, finds another man's slave on the path, in the fields, or in the forest, running away from his master, he is expected to capture him. But if he sells the slave that he has captured without having first shown him at market in his *negeri* for a period of 8 days daily, displayed to see if anyone recognizes him, or [if anyone] knows who the master is, so that he can be sent to his rightful owner, then the one [who captured him] is seen as having stolen that slave, and then there is no mercy shown. If, however, the rightful owner comes while the slave is sitting on display, or [sends] an incontrovertible message with adequate proof, and demands that [the slave] be retained, then he, as the one who found and seized him, is given besides his own expenses, 6 rigsdaler as finder's reward. But if //**273**// no owner of the slave appears before the 8 days have passed, then the finder can freely sell the [slave] he found, whenever and wherever he desires, and this with impunity, even if the owner appears later. But this form of justice applies only in the case of slaves, their most important possession. Other things that are found are not treated with such great trouble. And so it happens with slaves among the Negroes themselves: if a slave runs away from some European who thinks he can recognize his slave, then they are masterfully expert at casting doubt on his proof and marks of identification when they can. So their sense of justice is not nearly as great as it would appear, or indeed has been reputed, since unfaithfulness, swindling and thievery are among their most practised sins, as I have reported earlier.

On the 22$^{nd}$, towards evening, a gull flew in on our deck. It had the colour and size of a turtle-dove, but to our great surprise we became aware that she had only one leg, by nature, and there was found no sign, neither under nor outside the skin, of the [missing] leg. //**274**//

On the 26$^{th}$ we sighted the island Anna Bona. It belongs to the Portuguese. In circumference it is nearly 3 miles, and it is far healthier as regards the air than is the island St. Thomas. All the inhabitants were black; they had 3 larger *negerier*, or villages, and 3 so-called churches.

They all want to be seen as Roman Catholic Christians, even though there was not a person in the country who could read a single letter, nor had they had any teacher there for 7 years. On this island neither gold nor money nor *bussies* were [used as] currency, but for everything we purchased from them we had to pay with wrought iron objects and thin woollen or linen cloth. They practised christening of small children according to the Christian manner, and they christened them properly with only water and in the name of the Holy Trinity. I questioned some of the young to discover if they had any knowledge of Christianity. They only knew the Lord's Prayer in Portuguese, and managed to answer who had created them, redeemed and sanctified them, but of the other sacraments of the Romans' practice they knew nothing. Yet each one went around with his //**275**// rosary, and prayed by reciting an *Ave Maria*.That island is richly provided by nature with all manner of African fruits, especially pumpkins, melons, sour and sweet *oranie-ebler*, or bitter oranges, and tamarind.

And here I must include something about that fruit, tamarind, since there has not been an opportunity to tell about it earlier. That is because the wild tamarind trees are not usually seen in any great number on the Coast of Guinea, as far as I know, except at a lagoon that is under Skema, a small Dutch fort, about 30 miles above Christiansborg. In the mouth of that lagoon, where it runs out into the sea, there is scarcely 2 feet of water – and there they enjoy a particular delight in finding extremely large turtles every night – where I have seen tamarind trees both in great numbers and as large as the best oak trees in Denmark. They drop their fruit in such huge quantities on the ground at the lagoon that one could load and fill a large boat with it. Yet, there it was simply crushed underfoot in disdain //**276**// because there was too much of it, and neither people nor animals bothered to eat it, because it is sour, although it is a choice and excellent fruit. And, as I myself have experienced in the warm countries, I hardly believe any better remedy can be found, in a hurry, against an attack of fever and an inflamed stomach, than to take as much as 1 *qvintin* of tamarind, and then fast for half a day. In that way it always had the desired effect. [109]

---

109 One *qvintin* = 5 grammes.

The [wood of the] tamarind tree is dense and hard, like the pear tree – neither coarser nor lighter [in structure]. The fruit hangs out of the branches in pods, like the largest variety of beans, 3 or 4 stones in each pod. The leaves are somewhat larger than a pimpernel leaf, or more like a newly opened fern leaf. Under the tree there is comfortable shade.

Northeast of that island there is a very good harbour, and at a musket shot from land there is good anchoring ground. A little to the east there is a special watering-place, but otherwise water is, in fact, found close by the harbour; but it is better for cooking than for drinking. Nonetheless, they have //**277**// what is best to support life: millie, rice and malaget, and they have no other bread than yams and *kassau* [cassava].

This kind of plant, *kassau*, grows everywhere around the fortress, Christiansborg, but never does any creature partake at all of the leaves or stem as its food. This moves me even more to believe the Negroes' description of *kassau*, whose leaves are similar to those of hops, but are not as sharp as hops leaves. The stem is reddish and as thick as a large cabbage stem. The Negroes say that if anyone has a toothache, he should cut a small piece of the stem as long and wide as the tooth, or teeth, and let it lie for half an hour on the gum. The teeth then loosen so they can be removed with one's fingers. On these *kassau* bushes there grow lovely black, clear [*sic*] berries. Of these berries I prepared something for a monkey, which is the most certain test for a foreign man – and I would advise everyone not to be tempted by unknown fruits that it rejects – but the monkey spat out the fruit and screamed. From this I conclude that there must be a dreadful // **278**// and poisonous juice in them, but, when the dangerous juice is completely pressed out of the roots, and the roots are then dried and ground into flour, like millie, you can make bread of it, and eat it without danger, just as I ate it on Anna Bona. I have been told that it is almost the only bread that ordinary people and slaves enjoy on the islands in America, and it neither tastes bad nor disagees with you. But sifted rye and wheat flour come either from Europe or mostly from New England, Pennsylvania, Carolina and other English places in America.

I must not neglect to report that although the Negroes on the entire island of Anna Bona were originally slaves whom the Portuguese had bought in Angola – a kingdom in Africa where the people are normally big and strong and without physical defects. It has now so degenerated that among 1,000 people – which is now the least number of those living on the island – you scarcely find [sic] one tenth of them who have deformed legs, both the lower and upper limb, so that you assume that they must be badly afflicted by scurvy //**279**// or dropsy; but, when you talk to them about this and ask the reason for it, they answer that they were born that way.

We stayed on that island, Anna Bona, until 1 December, when, at 3 o'clock in the morning, we set sail from there, and it was almost decided by our commander and the ship's council that we would sail straight to Barbados, an English island in America, because of lack of bread. But after we had been provisioned from the other warship, *Marie Gallej*, with a sufficient supply of flour and bread, it was decided that we would continue our journey to old England in Europe without delay.

On the 16th of that month, when we were at 9 degrees north latitude, and we again took stock of our supplies of provisions, we found it impossible that they would last long enough to reach Ireland or England. So the entire ship's council agreed that it was necessary to set sail for West India, namely Barbados, which was promptly put into action.

# Chapter Thirty-six

Thus I come to the last year of my journey, the year **1713**, in which, trusting wholly in God's mercy, I would soon see //**280**// Europe – admittedly with a weak body – and everyone on the warship was healthy, with only a few exceptions.

On 3 January, when we were between 11 and 12 degrees north latitude, we sighted a ship but could not determine which land he belonged to, but we decided that it must be a pirate.

At 1 o'clock in the afternoon, on 8 January, we sighted Barbados, which is a flourishing island. Better Spanish oranges, both sweet and sour, I believe can scarcely be found anywhere than on Barbados. In my weakness I was permitted by my doctor – a Quaker and a man wonderfully experienced in the art of medicine, whose name was Joseph Gambol – to eat a couple of the sweet oranges daily for my refreshment.

On the 9th, at midday, we landed at Barbados, where our commander showed such great consideration for me, as a foreigner and unwell, that I was given quarters in a hostel belonging to a very fine man by the name of Joseph Vollen, where I enjoyed much unexpected hospitality.

After Jamaica Barbados is the best island that the English own in America, //**281**// not to speak of New England, Carolina, Pennsylvania, Virginia, etc. which are on the mainland and are provinces of the greatest importance. Barbados is, according to the information of the English, 25 English miles long and 16 English miles wide. In charge of the island there was a Governor – an impressive gentleman – who held court a little way outside of the city St. Michael. There are 3 towns on the island, but St. Michael is the most important, since the major part of the maritime trade – which is, in fact, more important than one might have supposed, and which runs the country – is centred in that city.

There is a multitude of Jews. That people alone generate 1500 pounds sterling annually in free trade. They are so numerous that they have 3 synagogues in that country, and although their trade costs them a great deal, they know how to manage it with great industry, so that there are to be found very wealthy people among them.

Among the English, even more wealth is found among the Quakers. There are a great many, and they carry on considerable trade in that country, as I //**282**// have noticed in several places, so that one might conclude that the lack of formality and circumlocution that that people practice in their daily relationships, combined with industriousness, give them greater opportunity to manage their businesses.

It is reckoned that, counting both old and young Christians living in Barbados, there are 12,000, who, for their domestic work and the cultivation of the earth, maintain more than 60,000 slaves. The air is very healthy, the inhabitants very good-natured, the earth unbelievably fertile, especially as regards sugar, ginger and indigo, with which, along with cotton, etc., many ships are loaded annually. But their rye and wheat flour, rice, tobacco, tar, masts, logs, both for [the building of] ships and houses, horses, cows, animals for slaughter, butter, tallow, etc. must for the most part be obtained from other countries, which are on the mainland of America.

According to what the inhabitants themselves say there are 500 sugar mills in the country, none of which could be established – with its house and all that belongs to it – for less than 1,000 pounds stl. Indeed, a plantation, as they call it, is said to cost 15-20 [thousand] pounds sterling; so a very moderate plantation, with land, //**283**// mills, houses, slaves, horses, asses and oxen, etc., can cost as much as 6-8,000 pounds yearly to maintain.

The inhabitants in Barbados are, in general, very wealthy, as they are in Jamaica and in other English countries in America; although at all their customs places they have as careful supervisors as at any other place, and they must indeed pay high customs fees. But this wealth comes from the inhabitants having the freedom to use the land as they best know how to, and can do; and that with their own ships they can sail and trade wherever in the world they wish to, [trading] with the fruits of their own land, which they have in abundance, while having to pay 4 percent to the Crown. The only exception is slave-trading, which is left to the English African Company. Yet in England, Jamaica and Barbados they use more than 60 ships, besides the Company ships, for this trade, provided that the ship owners first pay the Company 10 percent of the value of the cargo. The inhabitants there told me that they all lived very poorly, the earth lay fallow, the Company was in arrears, and the Crown received //**284**// no income, as long as the English monopoly lasted. But now, since it has been dissolved and free trade established in its place, both the Crown and the inhabitants can enjoy good profit from the land.

Since I was told the costs for eating and foodstuffs, [I found] that everything there is extraordinarily expensive. A pig usually costs 3 pounds sterling; a sheep 2 ½ pounds sterling; an ox 12 pounds sterling; a chicken 1 English shilling; but among all such things there is nothing nearly as expensive as a horse, which, in Denmark, could cost 24 rigsdaler but cannot be purchased there for less than 60 pounds sterling, which is 240 rigsdaler specie. Indeed, I have seen a horse there the like of which you could purchase in Denmark for 50 rigsdaler, that I was assured, under oath, cost 160 pounds sterling. Indeed, a goose would even be called expensive food since it can be purchased for no less than 3 kroner – and I cannot forget that I saw goslings there at the end of January.

This island is also well fortified with redoubts and batteries at all the places where it is felt to be necessary, to prevent other people //**285**// – who would like to conquer that excellent country, which could be well worth owning – from entertaining the desire to attack it.

The governor of that country runs a princely state in all respects, and in every case he practices a royal authority, which is absolutely necessary there.

On 28 January I was in one of the Jews' synagogues, and was shown the eternally burning so-called holy lamp, which they claim has been burning since ancient times; and they keep it so as a remembrance of the holy fire in the tabernacle in the Temple. There were also other chandeliers, but without lights. Their pulpit was like ours; their choir entirely separated from the rest of the synagogue, and [there were] some steps from the floor up to the altar, which was not especially decorated.

# Chapter Thirty-seven

On 8 February, at 5 o'clock in the evening, we sailed from Barbados, and were sent off from the fortress with 21 salutes, which the warship *Falmuth*, on which I was sailing, answered, and, in the Name of the Lord, set our course for Europe.

On the 10th of the same month, in the morning, //**286**// we sighted the French island Dominica, and by midday, [we saw] several other small islands to the west. However, the sea was so calm, and there was so little wind that we needed all the sails we could set in order to move forward.

The day after, the 11th, at midday, we sighted a small ship, which our commander challenged with live shot under the English flag and, at 2 bells in the afternoon, it came up alongside. Then we could see that the ship was from Glasgow in Scotland, heading towards Antigoa. That ship brought us the glad tidings that peace had been declared beween England and France.

We continued sailing, and felt the sea and increased winds more and more, until, on 14 Feb., because of this, we had to lower our top-gallant sail, stunsail, and stern sail, since the wind and weather made it impossible to use them any longer.

On the 16th, in the evening, we had a very severe storm, which grew stronger toward nightfall, until, on that same night, the yard on our main mast broke, for which we were totally unprepared. //**287**//

On the 17th, in the morning, according to our estimation, we passed the Tropic of Cancer, and on the same day, we set up a new yard to replace the one that had broken in the stormy weather we had had earlier. On the same day one of the sailors died quite suddenly.

On the 19th, at 28 degrees, there were 3 small whales playing around the ship. They were as large, and as broad as our sloop that takes 10 oars, but much longer. We could not but wonder at their energetic movements and daring in coming close to the ship.

On the 22nd, toward sunset, we sighted a sailer, sailing northwest, which our commander, with 2 live shots, challenged to come closer. He did not respond, but sailed due north, and was out of sight before 1 o'clock in the afternoon. For this reason we concluded that it must have been a pirate.

On 10 March, our main yard broke in a very severe storm from northwest. This was blowing for the second day, and still continued, so that it forced that strong, large ship into a state of industrious work, and us into a severe state of worry. //**288**//

On the 12th, at 8 o'clock in the morning, we took soundings and struck ground at 70 fathoms. By midday our main yard was finished [and could] replace the one that had broken. One must admit that that kind of work on ships is accomplished very quickly on the English ships in comparison to what is done on other ships. Our observation that day was 49 degrees 40 minutes. At 5 bells in the afternoon we sounded again and struck ground at 65 fathoms. That same evening we sighted a ship that we perceived belonged to England, and had a course toward Carolina in the West Indies [*sic*]. That ship informed us that we were 7 to 8 miles from the island Silly [Scilly], or Sorlings, which lies at the mouth of The Channel. //**289**// On 13 March, at 8 o'clock in the morning, we sounded again and struck ground at 65 fathoms again. That same day, between 10 and 11 in the morning, we sighted Silly Island north to east of us, and towards 2 o'clock in the afternoon we saw England. We also saw 2 ships, of which one was far away from us. We noted that it was an English ship, which may have come from France. The other one, which was closest to us, was a smaller ship. They informed us that it was based in Cork in Ireland and was bound for Lisbon. I could not but be amazed at the multitude of ships from England, with the sea fairly aswarm with them, as clear proof of the incredibly great trade that England is engaged in all parts of the world.

At 4 o'clock in the afternoon we sighted 4 ships. From the flags they were flying, as they showed their colours, we saw that the one closest to us was a Holsteiner; so the Second Lieutenant and I made ready and boarded him, since we realized that he was a hooker, coming from Bordeaux, and belonging to Fridriksort in Holstein.[110]

The day after, the 14 March, at //**290**// 8 o'clock in the morning – God be praised! – we anchored at Plejmouth's [Plymouth] Sound where I went ashore with the commander. We took our lodgings at Mr. Klarke's – a merchant and wine dealer there – where we were well taken care of after such a long journey. I looked around the place and found that Plejmouth might be smaller than Copenhagen by a quarter of the size, if you discount Christianshavn. The houses everywhere were old-fashioned buildings. There are 2 Reformed Churches, 2 Anabaptist, 3 Independent, 1 French church, 2 Jewish synagogues. The city itself is open, but has an extraordinarily strong fortress, built on a cliff; besides 3 smaller ones, all built on cliffs at the entrance to the city. About a bare half-mile west of the city there is a very safe, good harbour, where they have their cranes and works, and where there live such a great number of ships carpenters, ropemakers, wrights, sail makers, smiths and that kind of manual labourer, that they [each] have their own churches, and the place itself is approximately 3 quarters as large as all of Plymouth.

On the 20th, along with my host, //**291**// I went to see the Castle, which is very well fortified. It has its own church and minister. The cornerstone of that Castle is said to have been laid in 1666. All of the buildings are constructed of hewn granite boulders, and in the middle there is a green courtyard large enough for 4 regiments to be mustered easily. It must rightly be seen as an important fortress.

On the 25th I was at the yards at Plejmouth, where there were 2 second-rate war ships on stocks. There is an unbelievable supply of all manner of things required for ship-building. There have been assigned 2 masters from the Admirality to oversee everything at that place: from the paymaster, brewer, master of the arsenal, right down to the poorest labourer at the yards. They have free houses and living quarters conveniently built there. In the ropewalk – which is a house with a foundation – they can make the longest and largest anchor ropes that

---

110 A hooker is a fishing vessel; in this context probably a two-masted Dutch fishing vessel.

might be required. But in spite of all that can be found there, I was assured that at Portsmouth and Rattham there are larger and better yards.

On the 27<sup>th</sup>, at midday, we left //**292**// that harbour, and with a light breeze went out to sea, but the wind died down at night. Therefore, since it did not improve, we had to return in great disappointment.

On the 28<sup>th</sup>, at 4 o'clock in the afternoon, we anchored again in the sound outside of Plejmouth, and had to be satisfied that we could blame it on difficulty with the wind.

On the 29<sup>th</sup> I was in one of the small fortresses, which lies on a small island northwest of the Castle, but not farther out than they could, with a 6-pounder, easily reach the other one; so that not a single boat could go into the yards against their will. There is, in fact, an inlet between the smaller castle and My Lord Atskok's [?Ascot's] country estate, but at high tide it is only 4 – 5 feet deep, so the inlet and the sound can be kept clear by the smaller castle. And here I must insert something that was told to me about My Lord Atskok. He was said to be a member of the ancient English nobility, and that he held such a large, impressive estate that it brought him 7,000 pounds sterling annually. Further, that he lives in the country in an extraordinarily //**293**// beautiful house, that has as many windows as the year has days; as many doors as the year has weeks; as many chimneys as the year has months. I did not see it but a number of people have told me about it.

On 30 March, the Brandenburger Assistant Merchant, Mr. Jppe Olivier, who had been with us from the coast of Guinea, transferred from the warship *Falmuth* over to the Amsterdam ship, called the *Gyldne Morgenstjerne*, which had come to anchor the day before in Plejmouth's Sound, after a successful journey from Genua.

On 2 April, at midday, an English warship called *Foulkston* arrived – [armed] with 40 cannons; and the next day, the 3<sup>rd</sup>, in like manner, from Jamaika there came an English warship called *Defiens* [*Defiance?*] with 70 cannons. Both of them anchored alongside us.

On the 4<sup>th</sup>, at 10 bells in the morning, we sailed from Plejmouth. In a fleet with us were the above-mentioned *Defiens* and *Antelope*, an English warship with 50 cannons, as well as the aforementioned Dutch merchantman with 18 cannons. Towards 1 o'clock in the afternoon we were at the longitude of the Eddystone Light. //**294**// This is what a cliff in The Channel is called, upon which, at great cost and expertise there has been raised a lighthouse, where, every night, 6 lamps are lit for the seafarers. The royal magazine in Plejmouth gives the lighthouse keeper, besides his free board, a salary of 50 pd. st. annually, and he is said to live in that tower.

On 5 April, from 5 to 10 bells, we sailed along the coast of the island Wigth [Isle of Wight], which is more than 5 Danish miles long and 3 miles wide – a very rich and fertile land with three market places. At 11 o'clock in the morning we sighted Portsmouth, and anchored 2 miles below, so that we had Portsmouth north of us and Spitehead [Spithead] northeast.

On the 6th, in the afternoon, the warship *Falmouth* weighed anchor and went up to the road at Spitehead, where it was teeming with English warships and merchant ships, showing proof of the great naval might of England, which surpasses all of Europe.

On the 8th, a little past midday, we weighed anchor and intended to continue the journey, but in leaving we ran aground on a sandbank, and since [the damage] looked so extensive for this //**295**// large ship, and it looked as if it could not possibly leave without [further] damage, I considered leaving the ship, in order to have more time for my journey.

Thereupon, on the 9th, I made ready to leave the warship *Falmouth*, and with many thanks, took my leave of Mr. Riddle, the Commander of the ship. I went ashore at Portsmouth, which is a very lovely and important trading area, where it was very lively, and there was great activity in business and trading, both in the city and in the harbour.

The day after, the 10th, I travelled by freight carriage to London, and arrived at Peter's Field in the evening, where I stayed the night. From there, on the 11th, I arrived at midday, at Gotlimon, a small but lovely village; at 2 o'clock in the afternoon at Guiltfort, which is a small town but without sea trade since it lies so far inland, but is on the River Thames. Here the inhabitants – using largely prams since other boats cannot be used on the river – carry on a not inconsiderable trade by

bringing many types of grain and animal products to London daily.
//296//

On the 12th, at midday, I arrived in Kingston, which is a very lovely small town, much like Guiltfort as regards trade. Outside of that town, 4 days earlier, on 8 April, a provincial attorney was hanged for having committed murder. Along with him 5 outlaws were hanged, of whom there are more in England than in any other land in Europa. Everyone was talking about it, and all spoke of the great callousness and derision with which one of them went to his death. This is not strange among the English, since a number of them make it a point of honour to be inhumanly unreasonable. On the same day, at 5 o'clock in the afternoon, I arrived in London.

The day after, the 13th, I arrived at the home of Mr. Frans Boje, who, on 17 Aug. **1711**, had come as commander to Christiansborg in Guinea. I delivered letters from him, and greetings to his virtuous wife; [to] Madame Johanna Smith, and her pious mother and brother, Mr. Edvard Smith, Officer at the Customs House in London. I was received with much pleasure and unexpected hospitality, in that they offered me a place in their house, which, //**297**// with no little modesty, I had to accept. I stayed there until 18 May, when I left London.

On 14 April there came an express [message] from Utrech[t] to her Majesty, Queen Anna, formally announcing that peace had been declared and signed 4 days earlier in Utrecht, and treaties exchanged. Thereupon, immediately, the white banner of peace was raised from the tower and all the cannons there were fired as a public declaration of peace.

On 18 April I was in the synagogue of the Portuguese Jews, which is an impressive building, and in appearance much like the garrison church called the *Master Zebaoth's Church* in Copenhagen. Those Jews were celebrating Passover then, and before the service began they lit candles in 6 large chandeliers, and likewise in almost countless candlesticks around the church and the pulpit. Around the lectern, covered with green velvet, where their rabbi stood and read the service, there were 7 unusually large white wax candles. They sang a number of, in our judgement, not proper songs, which sounded quite unusual in my ears, but if they //**298**// sounded better in God's ears is a greater question. Their rabbi and the entire congregation, which is unbelievably large, turn their faces towards the east while they read their prayers. There were no women present during this Passover service, and all the men who were there wandered around here and there, wherever they wanted to, with hats on their heads, during the service. Many of the Jewish boys scrap and fight in that formal gathering, so that their so-called service is nothing less than a prayer meeting. And, without a doubt, I was able to see, from the rabbi himself and his entire comportment, that in his heart he was of a deeper conviction.

On the 30th a ship left from London, with its course for Guinea, with which I sent a letter to Mr. Frans Boje, Commander at Christiansborg, to inform him of the course of my journey. On the same day, in the afternoon, I spoke with Mr. Mag. Jørgen Ursin, Chaplain of the Danish congregation here in London, and, since some of the congregation had requested of me that I deliver a guest sermon, although I felt weak, //**299**// I requested, and received, Mag. Ursin's permission to do this.

On 30 April, which was the 2nd Sunday after Easter, I delivered a sermon in the Danish church in London, which is a lovely little church, and remains an eternal reminder of Mr. Mag. Iver Brink, who, with great industry, made possible this lovely building.

On 3 May I went up to see the Monument in London, which is a high, round tower, built in 1667, in memory of the Great Fire that the Roman Catholics had started the year before, showing extreme treachery towards the city. In this fire 13,000 houses were burnt to ashes. From the ground up to the top, where the building is flat on top with an iron railing around it – like the round astronomical tower near Trinity Church in Copenhagen, but not nearly as large – you climb up 365 steps. The climb up is far more strenuous and difficult than it is in the Round Tower in Copenhagen, where there are no steps.

On 5 May I was at the Tower in London, which is a very strong castle and of very large dimensions. There I was first shown //**300**// 2 stuffed lions that had died several months before. But a female lion, or lioness, that had lived there since she was a cub and had been raised in that same room, was still alive. I was also shown 3 or 4 other varieties of strange animals. After that I was taken to the armoury where I saw, in the first room, an enormously large number of all kinds of useful and useless hand guns hanging up in various arrangements. In another department I was shown, besides a collection of guns, in the middle of the room, statues of the English kings, all in armour and on horseback. Among them were 2 English princes, one of an age of 12 years, the other of 5 years, upon whom Richard the Third, when he was their guardian, had let the bed canopy fall down and thus suffocated them in their bed. Around those kings and princes there stood perfectly fashioned tall horses with riders on their backs, which represented their guard. In another large room I was shown an innumerable quantity of old spears, swords, halberds, war axes, long battle swords, coats of mail that the English //**301**// had seized from the Spanish long ago. At that same place I held in my hand one of the old Danish war clubs with which the Danes, when they were masters over England, intended to kill all the English men. But the English women, when they realized this, each fell upon her own man, who was Danish, and on that very day, which had already been fixed by them long before, destroyed all the Danes with those same clubs. Because of this, the Englishmen tell us, women in England are always shown the honour of giving them, in the streets and lanes, a place nearest the wall, which is continued to be a show of honour, and they always sit at the head of the table.

At the same place I was shown a broad axe with which the queen of England, named Anna – the mother of the famous Queen Elizabeth – and a count of England, had been decapitated. And a great deal more of such things that are preserved there, which I did not consider worth remembering.

In the lowest room of the armoury are displayed a good number of all kinds of metal and iron cannons, as well as fine firing mortars, many of which had been seized in war. //**302**// A number had been cast to honour royalty, such as the so-called 'Queen Elizabeth's pistols', which are 2 culverins, very artistically fashioned.[111] There were also metal cannons belonging to the Duke of Gloucester, son of the Right

---

111 A culverin is a small hand gun.

Honourable Prince George.[112] They were 9 very fine 2-pounders that he used for his practice. And many more of such things.

I also had the honour of seeing the crown jewels: 3 priceless crowns and 3 very precious sceptres; also the font of gold from which the members of the royal family had been christened from early times. There were also 2 very large and extraordinarily artistically worked silver pitchers – which must be considered masterpieces – and which were used on the formal occasion of the crowning of the presently reigning queen. Further, I was shown a replica of the Tower building in silver plate, on which there are 6 towers. Even more, I saw there an eagle made of gold, of which the neck can be unscrewed, and oil can be poured into the body of the eagle. Then, when the head is replaced, this oil is poured out through the beak into a large gold spoon, whose handle is set with costly diamonds. This is used by the Archbishop //**303**// of Canterbury to annoint and ordain all the English kings and queens on the day of their crowning.

On 6 May I was at St. James Castle, Her Majesty the Queen's official residence, and I arrived there precisely during morning prayers, which, after very beautiful music by the choir master and other selected singers, were led that day by the Bishop of Salisbury, 2 deacons and 2 royal preachers. The queen herself was in [private?] prayer that day; and after prayers one of the queen's companions – who was an acquaintance of my hostess – showed me around all the apartments, which are absolutely beautiful and marvelous.

In the queen's bedroom I was shown, among other precious things, 5 paintings: on one side the queen's most worthy parents; and on the other side the most honourable Prince George of Denmark, her majesty's own portrait, and that of their son, the Duke of Gloucester – which are all said to resemble them very closely. At the same place I was shown a water bowl of cast gold that is held between the forepaws of a lion and a unicorn – all of it //**304**// in gold – that was standing on a white marble table. On that occasion I could easily see the difference between Guinea, where the gold comes from but they know nothing

---

112 Prince George of Denmark (1653-1708) was the husband of Queen Anne. The Duke of Gloucester was the only one of their children who survived infancy.

of [how to work it?], and Europe where the gold is so decoratively and artistically worked.

After that I walked around the palace park or meadow, which is large and extensive, and is an inexpressively enjoyable place for walking. An arm of the River Thames flows through it, and in that water there are great numbers of swans, wild ducks, Spanish ducks and geese.

Later, in the afternoon, I rode out to Kensington, a castle King William had built for his enjoyment, and where most honourable Prince Georg of Danmark nearly always stayed, in his day.[113] There I was shown – among a multitude of costly things in every room and in the chamber where the blessed master died – a green velvet armchair, in which he was sitting when he died in his sleep. Behind the castle there is a very large and lovely garden, containing 10 beautiful fountains; and behind the garden there is a zoo containing a great number of white, brown, grey and speckled roe deer. This castle with its //**305**// adjoining garden and beautiful [surroundings] is far more excellent and more impressive than St. James.

I went over to Westminster, considered to be a separate city, although it lies closer to London than Christianshavn [does to] Copenhagen. There I saw the Hall first, which is an old-fashioned, much decorated building, where there is a stock market with all manner of merchants. It can, however, not be compared to the stock market in London, either as regards the building or the proper fittings, where on all weekdays during business hours can be found some 1,000 merchants from all manner of people and countries. From there I went to Westminster Church, which, in like manner, is a very old and especially artful building, unusually high and of great size. I was shown the royal sarcophagi behind the choir. There can be seen, one after the other, English kings, queens and princes, numbering some 100. On top of each grave is the year of death, and a full-sized image of the deceased, either in white marble or in metal. One coffin was opened for me, in which lay a queen of England who was said to have been dead for 200 years, and the body is still as good as whole and //**306**// complete, with the bones still covered by the natural skin. I noticed that among

---

113 This was King William III, Queen Anne's predecessor.

the deceased English kings there was one carved in white marble, and under the soles of his feet, on the soles of his shoes, there were carved out 2 monks who were reading the last rites while holding their rosaries in their hands. But now, in these days, they do not pray so devoutly for the English kings at their deaths, since by the English Reformation they lost some 1,000 cloisters and properties belonging to them

In another section of the same church I saw 2 ancient wooden chairs, like choir stalls [sic], upon which, from ancient times, all the English kings and queens sat when they were enthroned. On those chairs there is absolutely no decoration or anything unusual other than their extreme age.

I was also shown the Upper and Lower houses of Parliament and the House of Commons, and on the gable of the house of Parliament, the door, now sealed, through which the King, most honourable Charles Stuart I, was taken out by his furious subjects to be beheaded by the hand of the executioner //**307**// in 1649. I was also shown the cellar under the Houses of Parliament, in which Henry Garnetus, then the Prior of the Jesuit College in England, with his followers, had so secretely filled 36 barrels with gunpowder, and, to increase their effect had placed logs and stones over those barrels, with the intention of blowing up the building with the king and all the lords and members in Upper and Lower [Houses of] Parliament while they were sitting and conducting their affairs. But God, in his boundless mercy, let it be discovered in 1606 [sic], a short time before the terrible murders were to have taken place, as a remarkable proof of his special watch over governments.[114]

On 7 May I was in the Cathedral in London – called St. Paul's Church – which is an indescribably costly building, since the Englishmen appear to have wanted to compete with the Papists [to see] whether St. Peter's in Rome, or St. Paul's in London would win the prize. But since the pure teaching of God's Word adorns both of them they were equally impressive, since that is the true gold, silver and costly stones with which they are built. *I Cor*: 3.12. //**308**// Everything else, in comparison, is hay, straw and wood. They began to rebuild St.

---

114 Reference is to the Gunpowder Plot, 5 November 1605.

Paul's Church in 1676, after the earlier one had been burnt to ashes by the Great Fire. There were 4- to 500 men working on it daily, and there are still 100 men working there daily, [who will continue] for a good 10 years and more. Up to the present time it is said to have cost more than 2,200,000 pounds sterling, which is credible. The tower is in the middle of the church; its height from the floor to the top is 360 English feet. It cannot be imagined, for those who have not seen it, how enormous the building is, of which an eighth part would have been sufficient for the congregation and the services. Indeed, 4 ministers, if it were thus divided, could comfortably hold services, each for a large congregation, and not one of these would disturb the others. The official servants are the Bishop of London, 1 deacon, 2 chaplains and more, whose annual income is reckoned collectively to be 5,800 pound sterling – far more than what is paid here in Nordland. Underneath the church there is a room equally large but not as high as that above, 2 fathoms high everywhere, //**309**// which is designated for burials. The entire building, both above and below, is of square-cut stones, the floor is covered with black and white tiles; there are the loveliest images worked in stone, which can now be mounted, and nothing is spared in the way of [employing] artists. The iron railing, which circles the church grounds – whose foundation is of square-cut stones – is said to have cost 14,000 pounds sterling. The music in that church is always most excellent.

On 13 May an official messenger brought to the Queen of England the Ratification of the Peace between England and France.

On the 15th I saw a special fete, during which the women and girls who go around London selling milk, annually hold a great celebration. There were gathered more than 60, all with their straw or woollen hats, decorated with green ribbons. They went from house to house, with musicians ahead of them, and danced an English dance before every single door. But among them there was one who went around carrying on her head a milk bucket upon which there had been hung an entire net [full] of all manner of English official measuring cups of //**310**// silver. Above the quarts and pints that were set up like a pyramid, there was a large silver bowl, around whose entire edge there hung a good number of gold chains, diamond jewellery, gold watches and other such precious things. This May Countess had a number of men around her for her protection.

On the day after, the 16th there was a greater celebration, since on that day the peace treaty between England and France was announced. As soon as the Lord Mayor and the 24 Aldermen of London had received the document from the Queen's hand at St. James, all the cannons on the warships around the Tower saluted 3 times; after which the Lord Mayor and the above-mentioned aldermen mounted horses, all [the men] in beautiful clothing and decorated sumptuously. After them rode the herold, and after him, on horseback, came 2 drummers and 12 trumpeters, and after them 24 of the guard. In that order they rode first to the stock market, where the peace had first been made known; thereafter they moved to other public places, to announce the same glad tidings. Meanwhile bells were heard ringing, and choirs [singing] in all the churches from 12 midday //311// until 12 at night. As soon as it became dark, besides bonfires on every corner of every street and lane, all the houses were illuminated, so that one could see nothing but fires of celebration. And on that night the weather was so calm that they hung lights out, under the open sky, on all the balconies, as well as on the paths which are commonly used around the houses out to the streets, so that everywhere, in the entire city, there was great and shining joy.

By then I had stayed in London long enough, and seen wonderful things in abundance. Thus, on 18 May, at 5 o'clock in the afternoon, with an English ship called *Unity* – under Captain Robert Lister – I left London, and saw on that journey the incomparable length and size of that city, which is truly impressive.

On the 19th, at 3 o'clock in the morning, we arrived at Gravesant [Gravesend], which is an especially lovely little city, with truly costly and ornamented buildings. At 12 o'clock on the same day we arrived at Aalfornæs on the River Thames, where, because of a headwind we had to cast anchor. On that occasion I had the opportunity of observing 4 beautiful war ships, the first one //312// with 50 cannons, the second one with 44, the third one with 40 and the smallest one with 36. They lay there for the same reason that we had to anchor there. His Czarist Majesty had purchased them in England and they were to sail via the Baltic Sea.

On the day after, the 20th, at 6 o'clock in the morning, we weighed anchor with good weather and a south-wester, and, at 9 bells, met 5 English merchant ships that had come from Falmuth, all loaded with pewter. At midday more than 40 English ships, bound for London, all loaded with pit coal.

On the 23rd, at the Dogger Bank, the wind died down completely, and we set about fishing. There we caught wonderfully large, tasty cod. Towards evening we sailed away from there.

Finally, on 25 May, at 9 o'clock in the morning, from the masthead we sighted Skagen's land and church. At midday we met the entire Dutch Baltic Sea fleet of 56 ships with a convoy of 4 warships. Towards night the northwest wind blew quite heavily and increased more and more through the night. This worried us not a little, particularly since the Swedes, //313// in the time of war, did not light the lighthouses at the usual places and we found ourselves, then in [a state of] disrepair, between Niddingen and Kulden.[115]

But God also made that danger disappear, since, on 26 May, at 11 o'clock in the morning, we anchored in Øresund [The Sound], whereupon I immediately took my leave of the English ship, and was set ashore. Just there I found a freight boat lying ready to go up to Copenhagen. At 4 o'clock in the afternoon, Lord be praised, in only fair health, I arrived back in my fatherland, 4 years and 5 months after I had left it. I had seen many of God's wonderful deeds – testimonials to his great power – and observed so much of the blindness of the heathens to make me wonder at God's indescribable patience. I had found powerful salvation from many dangers to preach the Lord's fidelity. Could I write to the honour and praise of God, as his benefactions deserve, or even just because my heart is filled with gratitude, then I would write very extensively. These things described here, which I have noted during my journey, //314// I have felt that I owed to others to become informed,

---

115 Niddingen is a cliff in the skerries off Gothenberg; Kullen is a projecting, sharp rock north in The Sound.

so I could encourage others to join me in praising and glorifying God's wonderful might, wondrous patience and great fidelity. This I must do even more since God has let me see how many thousands of people there are who do not know God. If I achieve this goal among some, then I shall gladly lay down my pen, and in all honesty commend my readers to God's mercy and charity!

# Bishop Nannestad's Epilogue

[314] Now, in conclusion, to give the favourably disposed reader a somewhat more detailed report about that worthy man, who has described with such diligence and indefatigable constancy those things he had recorded on his journey to and from Guinea, and his having noted and remarked upon things that happened during his service at Christiansborg Fortress, at that same place; and since it is expected that one who has now read through this and, it is our wish, has found pleasure in it, would have gleaned from these pages something of the man's condition of life during the few years spent outside his Fatherland, [315] [that one] would also find pleasure in a glimpse of his entire life presented in a few words, showing that with God's good, providential eye watching over him, he was protected both at home and on foreign shores. Thus, that both the favourably disposed reader's desire can be satisfied, but also that he not be bored by an extensive description, it is here presented, very briefly, his life's beginning, progress and exit.

This very honourable and well-educated man of God, Mr. Johannes Rask, formerly minister and evangelical instructor for the parishes at Norstad and Kæringøen, was born at Halstæd vicarage on Laaland, in the year 1678, on 20 February. His father was the highly honourable and much learned man Mr. Mag. Johannes Rask, minister at Nørreherred and vicar at Halstæd and Avnede parishes on Laaland [ in Denmark]. His mother was Sara Ferøe.

By these Christian parents he was, at an early age, and in their own home, industriously guided and instructed in the knowledge of the Lord and the path of virtue. This continued [316] later in the public school in Nykøbing, where he was instructed in the Scriptures;

and also by the praiseworthy diligence, at that school, of the highly respected and well-known, learned man, Mag. Peter Højelse; by whom the young Johannes Rask, at the age of 19, in the year 1697, was sent with a good report from the school in Nykøbing to the High School in Copenhagen. There, with great willingness to learn, he continued his studies, and, with desired progress, he stood for all his examinations with satisfactory competence, as the laws demand of the students, by which the officially presented testimonial can provide the most reliable information.

Then, on 6 October 1708, he was appointed by the Director of the Royal Chartered West-Indian and Guinea Company to be the garrison chaplain at the Fortress Christiansborg in Guinea. This was verified by the Royal Most Merciful document of his calling on 19 October. After that, on 31 October, he was ordained in his calling by Bishop D. Henrik Bornemand. [**317**]

In the Name of the Lord, on 5 December, he embarked on the journey to Guinea, the progress of which has been described in the foregoing pages; and with God's merciful accompaniment, he arrived in good health at Christiansborg in Guinea, on 25 April 1709. There, for a period of 2 years, with good health and all possible diligence in constant prayer, and always preaching the Word, he harvested the fruit of God's blessing in the practice of his calling. However, the 3$^{rd}$ year brought him, who could not tolerate the hot climate, constant weakness to his body, because of which he was forced to seek his resignation, which he was granted with all the honour he could desire, as was his due for duties well-performed, on 26 September 1712, by Governor Frans Boje and the entire Council at Christiansborg. And after he had, with great emotion, accompanied by sorrow on both sides, taken his leave of the beloved congregation for which he had been responsible hitherto, in the Name of the Lord, he embarked upon his journey home in the evening of 29 September. Finally, on 7 November, he left Africa, where he had been living for 3 years, and had seen God's deeds, [**318**] in particular those described in this small script, along with much more that he observed for his own edification.

The following year, 1713, on 9 January, he arrived in America, or the so-called New World. Here he did not neglect either to take note, with keen attention, of what he saw; or to write down, industriously, what he considered worthy of note, as can be seen in the foregoing script. After a month's time, on 8 February the same year, he left America for Europe, another part of the world.

In the same year, 1713, on 26 May, with many thanks to God, he finally arrived in Copenhagen, and there, after having given his oral report to the West-Indian Company's directors, with the help of doctors, he recovered from his weakened health condition.

Finally, the following year, 1714, on 22 October, he was most humbly called to be the minister for the congregations in Foldernæs, Rørstad and Kæringøe in Salten Deanery in Nordland, in the diocese of Trondheim [in Norway]. But since winter was at hand, he had to delay his journey until the next year, so, on 18 June 1715 he arrived to undertake his living, [319] brought by God's Omniscient Providence and Direction, so far north, to test the extreme cold of this place, just as he had experienced the sun's almost unbearable rays in the world's southernmost areas earlier. Yet, he tolerated the cold of the north with stronger health than he had done in the heat of the south, which he had scarcely been able to tolerate for 2 years. But here in the north his constant and industrious work in God's work ameliorated the cold for him; since he filled his position with such faith and precision, and was therefore rewarded with God's powerful support to harvest the fruit of his great work for the LORD. Thus the Merciful God blessed him in his home with an amiable wife and a beloved son, Johan Georg Rask, who later, when his father, Mr. Johannes Rask, had been working in his calling for more than 28 years, became his father's helper in his old age. Thus, in 1742, Mr. Johannes Rask called the above-named son, Johan Georg Rask, to be his assistant in his post, who was appointed thus on 5 July 1743. [320]

Thereupon, on 8 February 1744, it pleased the Eternal God to put an end, with a blessed death, to that faithful servant's great work, and to call him from this world's constant toil, to the eternal Sabbath rest; and after his extensive wanderings in many foreign lands and areas of the world here on earth, to bring him home to the sacrosanct kingdom and fatherland in heaven; after he had lived for 66 years less 12 days and had filled the post of minister in the south and in the north for 35 years and 4 months. His son, Mr. Johan George Rask, who had been his assistant for something over a year, became his successor in the position, in which he is still serving faithfully, to the honour of the Lord and the edification of the congregation.

# Bibliography

Andrewes, William J.H. *The Quest for Longitude*, Harvard 1996

Asare Opoku, Kofi *West African Traditional Religion*, Accra 1978

Boateng, E.A. *A Geography of Ghana*, Cambridge U.Press 1970

Daniell, William F. 'On the Ethnography of Akkrah and Adampe, Gold Coast Western Africa', *Journal of the Ethnological Society* 4 (1856) 1-32

Fage, J.D. 'Some remarks on beads and trade in Lower Guinea in the sixteenth and seventeenth centuries', *Journal of African History* 3 (1962) 343-7
– 'More about aggrey and akori beads' in *2000 Ans d'Histoire Africaine*, Paris (1981) 205-11
– *A History of Africa*, London 1995

Field, M.J. *Religion and Medicine of the Ga People*, London 1937, reprinted 1961

Isert, Paul Erdmann *Letters on West Africa and the Slave Trade (1788)* trans. and ed. S.A. Winsnes, British Academy, Oxford 1992; a paperback edition, Sub- Saharan Publishers, Legon-Accra 2007

Johnson, Marion 'The cowrie currency of West Africa' *Journal of African History* 11, 1970, 17-49, 331-53

Kalous, Milan 'Akorite. '*Journal of African History* 20 (1979) 203-217

Kyerematen, A.A.Y. *Panoply of Ghana*, New York 1964

Law, Robin *The Slave Coast of West Africa 1550-1750* Clarendon Press Oxford 1991

Nketia, J.H. *Our Drums and Drummers*, Accra 1968

Nørregård, Georg *Danish Settlements in West Africa 1658-1850*, Boston 1966

Quartey-Papafio, A.B. 'The Ga Homowo Festival', *Journal of the African Society* 19 (1920) 126-34

Rømer, L.F. *A Reliable Account of the Coast of Guinea (1760)* trans. and ed. by S.A. Winsnes, The British Academy, Oxford University Press 2000

Serle, William and Morel, Gérard *A Field Guide to the Birds of West Africa* London 1977

Sobel, Dava *Longitude* Harper Perennial, 1995

Tilleman, Erik *A Short and Simple Account of the Country Guinea and its Nature 1697*, trans. and ed. S.A. Winsnes, Madison 1994

van Dantzig, Albert *Forts and Castles of Ghana* Accra 1980

Wilks, Ivor *Akwamu 1640 – 1750* NTNU Trondheim 2001

# Personal Names

# SHIPS

# Index of Select Subjects